Computer Basics
Windows 7 edition

Prentice Hall
is an imprint of

Harlow, England • London • New York • Boston • San Francisco • Toronto • Sydney • Singapore • Hong Kong
Tokyo • Seoul • Taipei • New Delhi • Cape Town • Madrid • Mexico City • Amsterdam • Munich • Paris • Milan

PEARSON EDUCATION LIMITED

Edinburgh Gate
Harlow CM20 2JE
Tel: +44 (0)1279 623623
Fax: +44 (0)1279 431059
Website: www.pearsoned.co.uk

First published in Great Britain in 2010

ISBN: 978-0-273-73684-4

British Library Cataloguing-in-Publication Data
A catalogue record for this book is available from the British Library

Library of Congress Cataloging-in-Publication Data
Ballew, Joli.
   Computer basics with Windows 7 in simple steps / Joli Ballew.
         p. cm.
   ISBN 978-0-273-73684-4 (pbk.)
  1. Microsoft Windows (Computer File) 2.   Operating systems (Computers)   I. Title.
   QA76.76.O63B359237 2010
   005.4'46--dc22

10 9 8 7 6 5 4 3 2 1
14 13 12 11 10

Designed by pentacorbig, High Wycombe
Typeset in 11/14 pt ITC Stone Sans by 30
Printed and bound in Great Britain by Scotprint, Haddington, East Lothian.

Computer Basics
Windows 7 edition

in Simple steps

Joli Ballew

Use your computer with confidence

Get to grips with practical computing tasks with minimal time, fuss and bother.

In Simple Steps guides guarantee immediate results. They tell you everything you need to know on a specific application; from the most essential tasks to master, to every activity you'll want to accomplish, through to solving the most common problems you'll encounter.

Helpful features

To build your confidence and help you to get the most out of your computer, practical hints, tips and shortcuts feature on every page:

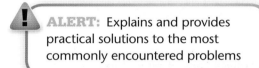 **ALERT:** Explains and provides practical solutions to the most commonly encountered problems

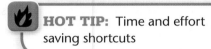 **HOT TIP:** Time and effort saving shortcuts

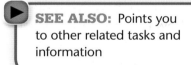 **SEE ALSO:** Points you to other related tasks and information

 **DID YOU KNOW?** Additional features to explore

WHAT DOES THIS MEAN?
Jargon and technical terms explained in plain English

Practical. Simple. Fast.

Dedication:

For you, dear reader; may you find your first steps into the world of computing both satisfying and rewarding!

Acknowledgements:

I love writing books for Pearson. Steve Temblett, Katy Robinson, Natasha Whelan and the rest of the gang are great to work with. They take my simple Word documents and meticulously edit, place and replace my text and images to produce a beautiful book complete with four-colour photos and easy-to-read pages. We've had a great run of titles and I hope to write more in the future. I am thankful for everyone at Pearson and the opportunities they've given me, and I am thankful for you, gentle reader, for putting your faith in me and my abilities to teach you something about computing (and hopefully whet your appetite for more).

I am thankful for many other things too, and I am fully aware of all of the blessings in my life. My 89-year-old father lives alone successfully even after my mom's passing a little over a year ago. He still drives, shops and makes his own decisions, making my life much easier than it could be were the situation any different. I myself have been blessed with good health and a great doctor, and at the age of 45, show no signs of slowing down. I have a wonderful family, including Jennifer, Andrew, Dad and Cosmo. We look out for each other and manage life day by day. We may be small but we're strong!

I am also thankful for my agent, Neil Salkind from Studio B and the Salkind Literary Agency. He always looks out for me, provides new opportunities, and forces me to think out of the box when it comes to new projects. There's always a new technology or gadget, a new publisher or a new book series to discover. Neil watches my back, and offers unconditional support. Even when I'm wrong, I'm right, at least in his eyes. I doubt many people have someone like that in their lives.

Contents at a glance

Top 10 Computer Basics Problems Solved

Contents

Top 10 Computer Basics Tips

1 Set up a PC or laptop

5 Work with windows

6 Personalise Windows 7

7 Surf the internet

8 Get Windows Live Essentials

9 Windows Live Mail

10 Work with media

11 Connect to your home network

12 Manage computer resources and connected devices

13 Stay secure

14 Fix problems

Top 10 Computer Basics Problems Solved

Top 10 Computer Basics Tips

Tip 1: Explore the Getting Started window

You'll see a Getting Started option on the Start menu. If you hover the cursor over it, you'll see a 'jump list' that allows you to access a specific 'Getting Started' task quickly. If you click Getting Started though, the Getting Started window will open.

1 Click Start, and click Getting Started (don't click any specific task in the jump list).

2 In the Getting Started window, browse the available features.

3 Click the arrow in the top pane to learn more about the feature selected.

SEE ALSO: Go online to get Windows Live Essentials is covered in Chapter 8.

? DID YOU KNOW?

When you click an item in the bottom pane of the Getting Started window, the top pane changes to reflect your choice.

Tip 2: Create a folder

Your personal folders will suit your needs for a while, but you may want to create folders of your own. You can create a folder on the desktop or inside other folders to hold information you access often.

1 Right-click an empty area of your desktop.

2 Point to New.

3 Click Folder.

4 Type a name for the folder.

5 Press Enter on the keyboard.

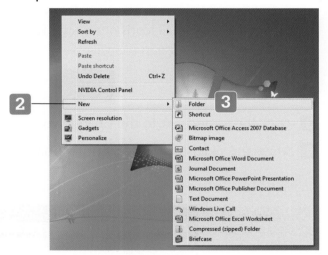

View	▶
Sort by	▶
Refresh	
Paste	
Paste shortcut	
Undo Delete	Ctrl+Z
NVIDIA Control Panel	
New	▶
Screen resolution	
Gadgets	
Personalize	

New ▶
- Folder **3**
- Shortcut
- Microsoft Office Access 2007 Database
- Bitmap image
- Contact
- Microsoft Office Word Document
- Journal Document
- Microsoft Office PowerPoint Presentation
- Microsoft Office Publisher Document
- Text Document
- Windows Live Call
- Microsoft Office Excel Worksheet
- Compressed (zipped) Folder
- Briefcase

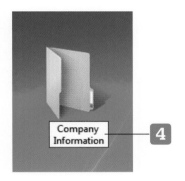

Company Information **4**

! ALERT: If you can't type a name for the folder, right-click the folder and select Rename.

? DID YOU KNOW?
You can drag the folder to another area of the desktop or even to another area of the hard drive to move it there.

🔥 HOT TIP: Create a folder to hold data related to a hobby, tax information, work or family.

Tip 3: Change the view in a window

When you open your personal folder from the Start menu or from the taskbar, you will see additional folders inside it. You open any of these subfolders to see what's inside them. You can change what their contents look like by changing how large or small their icons appear. You can configure each folder independently so that the data appears in a list, as small icons or as large icons, to name a few.

1 Click Start.

2 Click Pictures.

3 Click the arrow next to the Change your view button.

4 Move the slider to select an option from the list.

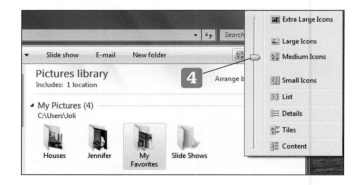

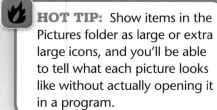

HOT TIP: Show items in the Documents window as Details to see the name of each document as well as the date it was created.

HOT TIP: Show items in the Pictures folder as large or extra large icons, and you'll be able to tell what each picture looks like without actually opening it in a program.

Tip 4: Change the desktop background

You can personalise the picture on the desktop to be just about anything you like. You can even choose from multiple 'backgrounds' and rotate them on a schedule.

1 Right-click an empty area of the desktop.

2 Click Personalize.

3 Click Desktop Background.

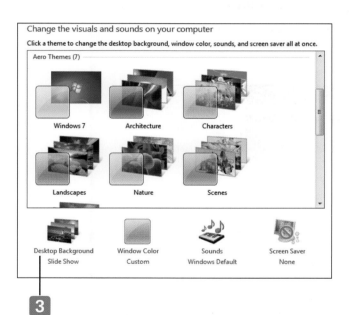

4 For Picture location, select Windows Desktop Backgrounds. If it is not chosen already, click the down arrow to locate it.

5 Use the scroll bars to locate the wallpaper to use as your desktop background.

6 Select a background to use or select multiple backgrounds as shown here.

7 Select a positioning option (the default, Fill, is the most common).

8 Select how often to change the backgrounds, if you selected more than one.

9 Click Save changes.

10 Click the red X in the top right corner of the Personalization window to close it.

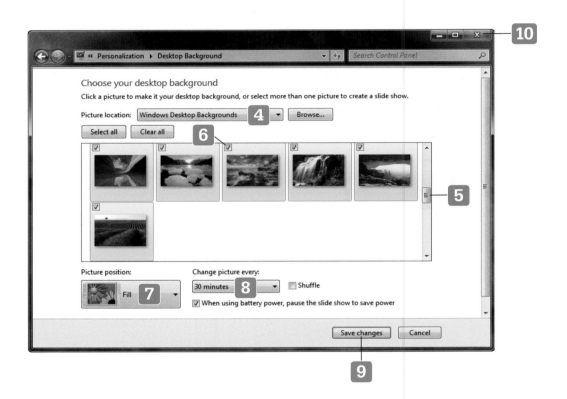

? DID YOU KNOW?

DID YOU KNOW?

You can click the Browse button to locate a picture you've taken, acquired or otherwise saved to your computer, and use it for a desktop background. Pictures are usually found in the Pictures folder.

Tip 5: Open a website in a new tab

You can open more than one website at a time in Internet Explorer. To do this, click the tab that appears to the right of the open webpage. Then, type the name of the website you'd like to visit.

1 Open Internet Explorer.

2 Click an empty tab.

3 Type the name of the website you'd like to visit in the address bar.

4 Press Enter on the keyboard.

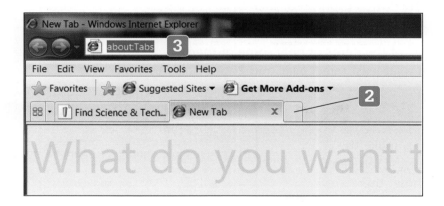

HOT TIP: Type the following:
http://www.microsoft.com/uk

DID YOU KNOW?
When a website name starts with https://, it means it's secure. When purchasing items online, make sure the payment pages have this prefix.

Tip 6: Download and install Windows Live Essentials

Windows Live Essentials contains all of the programs you'll need to manage email, instant message with contacts, edit photos, and even create and edit your own movies. You can choose to install additional applications from the suite too, including the Internet Explorer toolbar that connects all of this together seamlessly.

1 Open Internet Explorer and go to http://download.live.com/.

2 Look for the Download button and click it. You'll be prompted to click Download once more on the next screen.

3 Click Run, and when prompted, click Yes.

4 When prompted, select the items to download. You can select all of the items or only some of them. (Make sure to at least select Mail and Photo Gallery.)

5 Click Install.

6 When prompted to select your settings, make the desired choices. You can't go wrong here; there are no bad options.

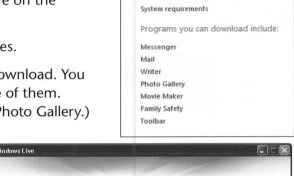

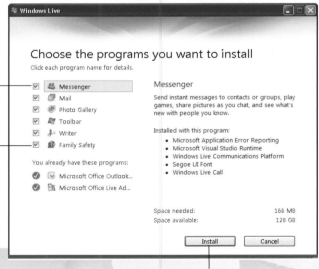

DID YOU KNOW?

It's OK to select all of these programs if you think you'll use them; they are all free.

HOT TIP: Select Mail, Photo Gallery and Toolbar for best results. You'll probably use all three.

Tip 7: Insert a picture directly into the body of an email

Windows Live Mail lets you add images to the body of an email and edit them before sending. You can even put 'frames' around them, have Windows 'autocorrect' colour and brightness, and add more photos easily. This is called a photo email.

1 Click New to open a new email.

2 Click Add photos.

3 Browse the photo(s) to add, and double-click them to add them.

4 Click any photo to add text, add a frame or rotate, among other options.

5 Complete the email, and when ready, click Send.

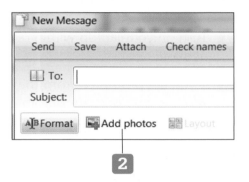

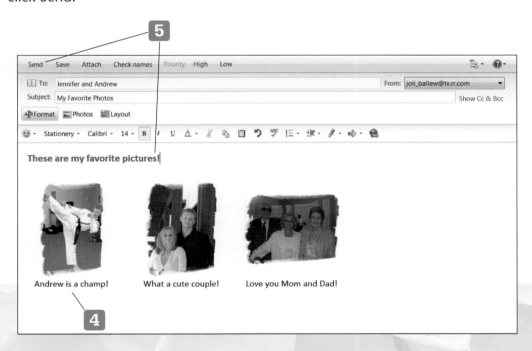

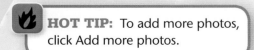

HOT TIP: To add more photos, click Add more photos.

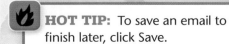

HOT TIP: To save an email to finish later, click Save.

Tip 8: Connect to a wireless network

You can use your laptop to connect to free Wi-Fi hotspots. Doing so lets you access the internet without physically connecting to a router or phone line, and without a monthly wireless bill. You can also use your laptop or desktop PC to connect to a wireless network you have at home or at work.

1 Turn on your laptop within range of a wireless network.

2 If you are prompted from the Notification area that wireless networks are available, click Connect to a network (not shown).

3 If you are not prompted to connect to a network, click the network icon in the Notification area.

4 If more than one wireless network is available, locate the one that you want to use and click Connect.

5 When prompted, choose the type of network you're connecting to (Home, Work, Public).

6 Input required security information, if prompted, and click OK.

network icon

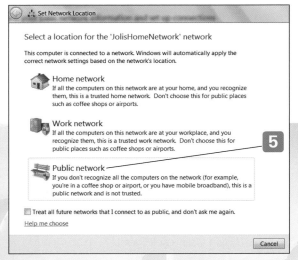

 HOT TIP: To find a Wi-Fi hotspot close to you, go to www.maps.google.com and search for Wi-Fi hotspots. You'll find them in various places including airports, hotels, bars, cafes, restaurants and more.

ALERT: Often you'll have to go into the building that offers the wireless connection, or sit right outside, perhaps in a patio area.

Tip 9: Use ReadyBoost

ReadyBoost is a technology that lets you add more RAM (random access memory) to your computer easily, without opening the case. Adding RAM often improves performance dramatically. ReadyBoost lets you use a USB flash drive or a secure digital memory card (like the one in your digital camera) as RAM, if it meets certain requirements.

1 Insert a USB flash drive, thumb drive, portable music player or memory card into an available slot on the outside of your computer.

2 Wait while Windows 7 checks to see if the device can perform as memory.

3 If prompted to use the flash drive or memory card to improve system performance, click Speed up my system.

 HOT TIP: Only newer and larger USB keys will work for ReadyBoost.

 ALERT: USB keys must meet certain specifications, but don't worry about that, you'll be told if the hardware isn't up to par.

Tip 10: Open Help and Support

Windows 7 offers lots of Help and Support files. You can search Help and Support as you would any website, by clicking a link, using the Back button, and even clicking the Home icon to return to the opening Help and Support page.

1 Click Start, and click Help and Support.

2 Click How to get started with your computer.

3 Browse the information in the resulting window to learn more about protecting your computer, what to do the first few weeks of owning one, and installing programs.

Help and Support

Not sure where to start? **2**
- How to get started with your computer
- Learn about Windows Basics
- Browse Help topics

HOT TIP: Your immediate priorities, after learning how to navigate your new computer, is to get online and connected to the internet.

DID YOU KNOW?
Windows 7 has an application that helps you transfer your files and settings from another PC, but we think it's best to transfer your data and configure your settings manually, as you'll learn in Chapters 4 and 6.

1 Set up a PC or laptop

Introduction

New PCs and laptops come with instructions for setting them up. If you have instructions, you should follow them. However, if you purchased a used computer or one was handed down to you, you probably won't have anything to guide you through the process, and the instructions that came with your new PC may not offer all of the information you need. Whatever the case, you can follow the instructions here. Once you've connected the monitor, mouse, keyboard and speakers, you can then concentrate on connecting and installing non-essential items like a printer, web cam, and other hardware, and getting to know a laptop's touchpad and the computer keyboard.

Locate and plug in the power cable

A power cable is the cable that you will use to connect your computer to the wall outlet (power outlet). Sometimes a power cord has two parts that need to be connected.

1 Locate the power cord. It may consist of two pieces that need to be connected.

2 Connect the power cord to the back or side of the computer as noted in the documentation. You may see a symbol similar to the one shown here.

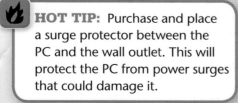

3 Plug the power cord into the wall outlet.

? DID YOU KNOW?

When you connect the power cable for a laptop, the laptop will use the power from the outlet and charge the battery at the same time. When you unplug the laptop from the power outlet, the laptop will run on stored battery power.

HOT TIP: Purchase and place a surge protector between the PC and the wall outlet. This will protect the PC from power surges that could damage it.

Connect the monitor

PCs come with a monitor that has to be connected. Older PCs use a connection like the one shown here, but newer PCs can have additional types of connection.

1 Place the monitor where desired, but within reach of the computer's tower.

2 Plug the monitor into a wall outlet so that it has power.

3 Locate the cord that connects the monitor to the PC and look at the end of it.

4 Find the compatible connection on the PC tower.

5 Make the connection.

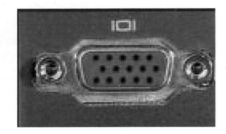

 HOT TIP: Most monitor connections plug into a compatible 'port' on the tower, and also have two screws for securing the connection.

 HOT TIP: The connection for the monitor shown here is the most common, but does not offer the best picture. If you have another type of connection on both your PC and your monitor (and the appropriate cable), use it.

Connect a USB mouse and keyboard

USB ports, or Universal Serial Bus ports, offer a place to connect USB devices. USB devices include mice, external keyboards, digital cameras and other devices.

1 Connect the mouse to an available USB port. It will only fit one way.

2 Repeat to connect the USB keyboard.

This laptop has two USB ports

 HOT TIP: If you are connecting a wireless keyboard and/or mouse, you'll need to sync them. Usually, you'll press a button on the USB 'dongle' and then a button on the mouse or keyboard.

 HOT TIP: If you received software with a keyboard and/or mouse, install it. The software will allow you to program the keyboard and use advanced features of the mouse.

Locate and press the Power button

Before you can use your computer or laptop you have to press the Power button to start the operating system. The operating system is Windows 7 and it allows you to use the computer.

1 If applicable, open the laptop's lid.

2 Press the Start button to turn on the computer.

? DID YOU KNOW?
Starting a computer is also called 'booting' it.

? DID YOU KNOW?
Most of the time the Power button is in the top centre of the keyboard on a laptop, or on the front of a PC tower for a desktop.

! ALERT: It takes a minute or so for the computer to start. Be patient!

! ALERT: If you ever have trouble starting Windows 7, during the boot-up process hit the F8 key on the keyboard. You can then choose from various start-up options, like 'safe mode'.

Activate Windows 7

If this is your first time starting Windows 7, and you're on a new computer, you'll be prompted to enter some information. Specifically, you'll type your name as you'd like it to appear on your Start menu (capital letters count) and activate Windows 7.

1 Follow the directions on the screen, clicking Next to move from one page of the activation wizard to the next.

2 When you have activated Windows 7, wait a few seconds for Windows 7 to initialise.

3 Click the Start button at the bottom of the Windows 7 screen to view your user name.

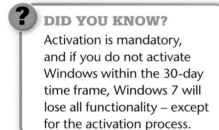

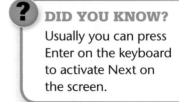

? DID YOU KNOW?

Activation is mandatory, and if you do not activate Windows within the 30-day time frame, Windows 7 will lose all functionality – except for the activation process.

! ALERT: To activate Windows 7 during the initial set-up, you'll have to be connected to the internet. Alternatively, you can use the phone number provided to activate over the phone.

? DID YOU KNOW?

Usually you can press Enter on the keyboard to activate Next on the screen.

Connect external speakers or headphones

If there are any external sound ports, you'll probably see three. Most of the time you have access to a line-in jack, a microphone-in jack and a headphones/speaker/line-out jack.

1 If necessary, plug the device into an electrical outlet.

2 Insert the cables that connect the device to the computer using the proper port.

3 If necessary, turn on the speakers or other device.

4 If prompted, work through any set-up processes.

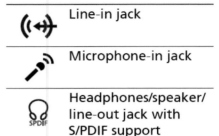

	Line-in jack
	Microphone-in jack
	Headphones/speaker/ line-out jack with S/PDIF support

WHAT DOES THIS MEAN?

A line-in jack: Accepts audio from external devices, like CD players.

A microphone-in jack: Accepts input from external microphones.

A headphone or speaker jack: Lets you connect your computer to an external source for output, including but not limited to speakers and headphones.

 DID YOU KNOW?

Line-in jacks bring data into the computer; line-out jacks port data out to external devices like speakers or headphones.

Connect and install a printer

Most of the time, to install a printer you insert the CD that came with the printer, plug it in and turn it on, and wait for Windows 7 to install it automatically. However, it's always best to have directions for performing a task, so in that vein, I've included them here.

1 Connect the printer to a wall outlet.

2 Connect the printer to the PC using either a USB cable or a parallel port cable.

3 Insert the CD for the device, if you have it.

4 If a pop-up message appears regarding the CD, click the X to close the window.

5 Turn on the device.

6 Wait while the driver is installed. If you're using Windows 7, you'll see what's shown here.

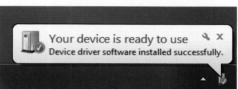

 ALERT: It's usually best to connect the new printer, turn it on and let the operating system (OS) install it. You only need to intervene when the OS can't install the printer on its own.

 DID YOU KNOW? USB is a faster connection than a parallel port, but with a printer, you probably won't notice a difference either way.

 ALERT: Read the directions that come with each new device you acquire. If there are *specific instructions* for *installing the driver*, follow those directions, not the generic directions offered here.

 ALERT: If the printer does not install properly, refer to the printer's user manual.

 DID YOU KNOW? Leave the CD in the drive. If the computer wants to access information on the CD, it will acquire it from there.

Connect and install a webcam

You install a webcam the same way you install a printer. You insert the CD that came with it, plug it in and turn it on, and wait for the operating system to install it. However, it's always best to have directions for performing a task, so in that vein, I've included them here.

1 Insert the CD for the device, if you have it, and close any windows that open as a result of this action.

2 Connect the camera to a wall outlet or insert fresh batteries.

3 Connect the camera to the PC using either a USB cable or a FireWire cable and turn it on.

4 Wait while the driver is installed.

 ALERT: If the camera does not install properly, refer to the user manual.

 DID YOU KNOW?
Leave the CD in the drive. If the computer wants to access information on the CD, it will acquire it from there.

 DID YOU KNOW?
FireWire is faster than USB.

For a laptop: locate, insert or remove the battery

Laptops have batteries, and they don't ship with them installed. You have to install the battery yourself. The battery is what allows you to use the laptop when not connected to a power source, and it must be charged prior to use.

 1 If the computer is turned on, turn it off.

2 Unplug the laptop from the wall outlet and remove the power cable. Set the power cable aside.

3 Carefully turn the laptop upside down and place it on a desk or table.

4 If applicable, locate the battery bay and open it.

5 If applicable, unlatch the battery latch.

 **SEE ALSO:** Shut down Windows safely, Chapter 2.

6 Insert the battery and lock the battery into place.

7 Secure the latch and, if applicable, close the battery bay door.

? **DID YOU KNOW?**
Some batteries, like the one shown here, don't use a battery bay, they simply click into place on the outside of the laptop.

WHAT DOES THIS MEAN?

Battery bay: This holds the computer's battery. Sometimes you have to use a screwdriver to get inside the battery bay, other times you simply need to slide out the compartment door.

Battery release latch: This latch holds the battery in place, even after the battery bay's door has been opened. You'll need to release this latch to get to the battery.

Battery lock: This locks the battery in position.

Connect additional hardware

For hardware other than printers or cameras, you'll need to insert a driver CD if one came with the hardware, plug in the new hardware and turn it on, and wait for the computer to install it.

1 Connect the hardware to the PC and/or a wall outlet.

2 Insert the CD for the device, if you have it.

3 If a pop-up message appears regarding the CD, click the X to close the window.

4 Turn on the device, if applicable.

5 Wait while the driver is installed.

ALERT: If the hardware does not install properly, refer to the user manual.

ALERT: On occasion, hardware manufacturers will require you to install software first, so read the instructions that came with your hardware to know what order to do what, just as a precaution.

Use the touchpad on a laptop

When you open a laptop for the first time, you'll probably see a device for moving the cursor, usually a touchpad. You'll use this to move the cursor around the screen.

1 Place your finger on the touchpad and move it around. Notice how the cursor moves on the screen.

2 If there are buttons, for the most part, the left button functions the same way the left button on a mouse does.

3 The right button functions the same way as the right button on a mouse does.

4 If there is a centre button, often this is used to scroll through pages. Try clicking and holding it to move up, down, left or right on a page.

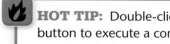 **HOT TIP:** Double-click the left touchpad button to execute a command, and click once to select something.

HOT TIP: Click the left touchpad button and hold it down while simultaneously moving your finger across the touchpad to select text.

HOT TIP: Click the right touchpad button to open contextual menus to access Copy, Select All and similar commands.

Locate specialised keyboard keys

Most computer keyboards have more than a few universal keys, and much of the time, these keys offer the same things across makes and models. For instance, pressing F1 (or the Windows key + F1) almost always opens a Help window for the open application.

1 With the computer turned on and running, press the F1 key. Note what happens; most probably the Help window will open.

2 Press the Windows key. This often opens the Start menu.

3 Press the F3 key. The Search window will probably open.

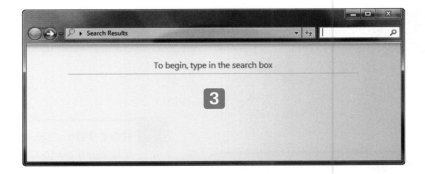

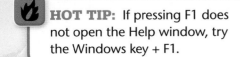

HOT TIP: If pressing F1 does not open the Help window, try the Windows key + F1.

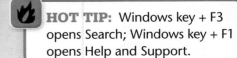

HOT TIP: Windows key + F3 opens Search; Windows key + F1 opens Help and Support.

2 First steps

Introduction

In the first chapter you learned how to connect a monitor, mouse and keyboard to your computer and turn it on. You also learned how to activate Windows 7 and install hardware like printers and webcams. Now, with your computer and hardware set up, you're ready to learn a little about Windows 7. You'll need to know how to get information about your computer, how to use the Getting Started window, how to use Help and Support, how to open and close applications and windows, and how to shut your computer down safely when you're ready for a break, among other things.

Know your computer specifications

There may come a time where you have to speak to a tech-savvy friend, Internet Service Provider (ISP) representative or other help desk technician. Those people will ask the same questions: 'What edition of Windows 7 are you running?'; 'How much RAM do you have?'; 'Is there anything called out in Device Manager, denoting a problem with your hardware?' Here's how to find the answer to those questions.

1 Click Start and locate Computer.

2 Right-click Computer and click Properties.

3 Review the information in the System window, including the Windows edition and amount of RAM.

4 Click Device Manager.

5 Note any 'unknown devices'. These devices are not currently recognised by Windows 7. A technician or tech-savvy friend can help you resolve any errors here.

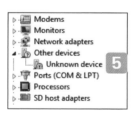

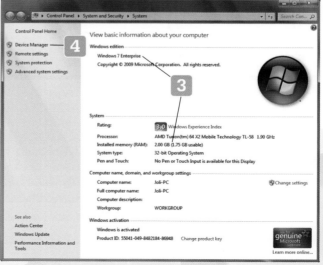

HOT TIP: Click the red X in the top right corner of the System window to make it disappear (i.e. to close the window).

Explore the Getting Started window

You'll see a Getting Started option on the Start menu. If you hover the cursor over it, you'll see a 'jump list' that allows you to access a specific 'Getting Started' task quickly. If you click Getting Started though, the Getting Started window will open.

1️⃣ Click Start, and click Getting Started (don't click any specific task in the jump list).

2️⃣ In the Getting Started window, browse the available features.

3️⃣ Click the arrow in the top pane to learn more about the feature selected.

? **DID YOU KNOW?**

When you click an item in the bottom pane of the Getting Started window, the top pane changes to reflect your choice.

▶ **SEE ALSO:** Go online to get Windows Live Essentials is covered in Chapter 8.

Open Help and Support

Windows 7 offers lots of Help and Support files. You can search Help and Support as you would any website, by clicking a link, using the Back button, and even clicking the Home icon to return to the opening Help and Support page.

1 Click Start, and click Help and Support.

2 Click How to get started with your computer.

Help and Support

3 Browse the information in the resulting window to learn more about protecting your computer, what to do the first few weeks of owning one, and installing programs.

Not sure where to start?   2

- How to get started with your computer
- Learn about Windows Basics
- Browse Help topics

 DID YOU KNOW?
Windows 7 has an application that helps you transfer your files and settings from another PC, but we think it's best to transfer your data and configure your settings manually, as you'll learn in Chapters 4 and 6.

HOT TIP: Your immediate priorities, after learning how to navigate your new computer, is to get online and connected to the internet.

Open an application

An application is a program that allows you to perform a task, like viewing a photo or playing a game. There are lots of applications included with Windows 7, including Notepad for writing letters, Calculator for performing mathematical calculations, Windows Media Player for listening to music and watching DVDs, and Paint for editing images or creating print-outs or signs.

1 Click Start.

2 Click All Programs.

3 If necessary, use the scroll bars to browse the applications.

4 Click Windows Media Player to open the application.

5 Repeat Steps 1, 2 and 3 to open additional applications: Desktop Gadget Gallery, Internet Explorer and Windows Update.

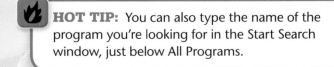

ALERT: To use an application you must first locate it, and then open it.

HOT TIP: You can also type the name of the program you're looking for in the Start Search window, just below All Programs.

Close an application

You can close an application by clicking the red X in the top right corner of the application or you can click the File menu (or Office button) and click Close or Exit.

1 In an application such as Media Player, Desktop Gadget Gallery or Internet Explorer, click the red X in the top right corner of the application window to close it.

2 In an application like Word or PowerPoint, click the Office button, and then choose Exit or Close, as applicable.

 HOT TIP: You won't be prompted to save changes in programs like Media Player and Internet Explorer; any changes you make here will automatically be saved by the operating system.

? DID YOU KNOW?
If you've made changes to a document, presentation or other data you'll be prompted to save the data when you close the program.

Open a window

Each time you click something in the Start menu, All Programs menu or on the Desktop, a window opens to display its contents. The window will stay open until you close it.

1 Click Start and click your user name.

2 View the items in your personal folder.

Close a window

To close a window, click the red X in the top right corner of it.

1 Click Start.

2 Click your user name. Your personal folder opens.

3 Click the X in the top right corner to close it.

4 All windows have a red X, even programs like the Desktop Gadget Gallery.

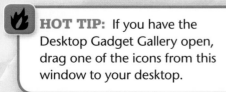

HOT TIP: If you have the Desktop Gadget Gallery open, drag one of the icons from this window to your desktop.

Search for a program with the Start menu

To locate a program on your computer you can search for it using the Start Search window. Just type in what you want, and select the appropriate program from the list.

1 Click Start.

2 In the Start Search window, type Photo.

3 Note the results.

4 Click any result to open it. If you want to open Windows Photo Gallery, click it once. Note that it's under Programs.

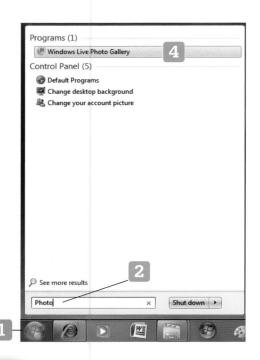

Programs (1)
- Windows Live Photo Gallery **4**

Control Panel (5)
- Default Programs
- Change desktop background
- Change your account picture

See more results **2**

Photo   ×   Shut down ▶

1

? DID YOU KNOW?
The Start Search feature became available in Windows Vista and is included with Windows 7, but was not available in Windows XP.

! ALERT: When you search using the Start Search window, all kinds of results may appear, not just programs.

HOT TIP: The easiest way to find something on your computer is to type it into this search window, and that includes files, folders, photos, music, pictures and videos.

Shut down Windows safely

When you're ready to turn off your computer, it's best to do so using the method detailed here. While some computers will 'go to sleep' after a specific period of time, they do not shut themselves off. When you're ready to shut down Windows, you'll need to do it this way.

1 Click Start.

2 Click the arrow next to Shut Down to see all of the options.

3 Click Shut Down. (Note that you can simply click Shut Down without clicking the arrow.)

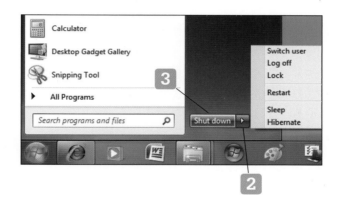

? DID YOU KNOW?

Some computers (and most laptops) come with a Sleep button. Clicking the Sleep button puts the computer to sleep immediately. If you're taking a break, you might want to try that now instead of completely shutting down the PC.

3 Explore Windows 7 applications

Introduction

You're probably ready to get started! You already know a little about the Start menu, and in this chapter you'll use the Start menu to access tools like the calculator and applications like Notepad. Once in Notepad, you'll learn how to write, save and print a letter, and then save the documents you create. You can apply what you learn here to other programs, including WordPad, Microsoft Office Word, Microsoft Office PowerPoint and others. Finally, you'll locate games, play Solitaire and view and empty the Recycle Bin.

Write a letter with Notepad

You can use Notepad to type a quick memo, note or letter. You can access Notepad from the Start menu.

1 Click Start.

2 In the Start Search window, type Notepad.

3 Click Notepad under Programs.

4 Click once inside Notepad, and start typing.

5 To change the font or font size, select the typed text and click Format, and then Font.

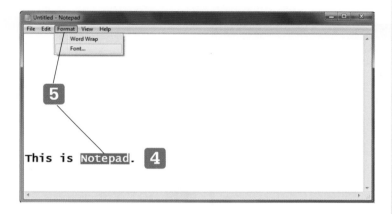

DID YOU KNOW?
Notepad has five menus: File, Edit, Format, View and Help. You can use these menus to save a letter, choose a font and more.

HOT TIP: Notepad's menus and dialogue boxes are similar to what you'll see in other programs, so it's a good idea to familiarise yourself with this program.

Save a letter with Notepad

If you want to save a letter you've written in Notepad, you have to click File and then click Save. This will allow you to name the file and save it to your hard drive. The next time you want to view the file, you can click File and then click Open.

1 Click File.

2 Click Save.

3 In the left pane, click Libraries.

4 Then, double-click Documents.

5 Type a name for the file.

6 Click Save.

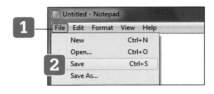

HOT TIP: If you don't see what's shown here, click Browse Folders. (Note that Hide Folders is showing in this screenshot.)

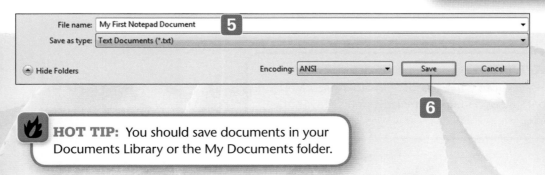

HOT TIP: You should save documents in your Documents Library or the My Documents folder.

Reopen a saved file

You can reopen saved files easily. Just locate the file in the Documents Library or My Documents folder and double-click it.

1 Click Start.

2 Click Documents.

3 Double-click the file to open it.

DID YOU KNOW?

If you save a file in the Documents Library it will also appear in the My Documents folder (and vice versa).

Print a letter with Notepad

Sometimes you'll need to print a letter so you can mail it. You can access the Print command from the File menu.

1 Click File.

2 Click Print.

3 Select a printer.

4 Click Print.

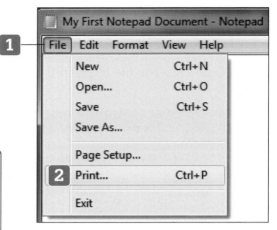

HOT TIP: You have to have a printer installed, plugged in and turned on to print.

WHAT DOES THIS MEAN?

Printer Preferences: Lets you select the page orientation, print order and the type of paper you'll be printing on, among other features.

Page Range: Lets you select which pages to print.

Use the Calculator

You've probably used a calculator before, and using the Windows 7 calculator is not much different from a hand-held one, except that you input numbers with a mouse click, keyboard or a number pad. There are four calculator options: Standard, Scientific, Programmer and Statistics. The Standard calculator is the default, and is a bare-bones version. The other versions offer many more features.

1 Click Start.

2 In the Start Search dialogue box, type Calc.

3 In the Programs results, click Calculator.

4 Input numbers using the keypad or by clicking the on-screen calculator with the mouse.

5 Close Calculator by clicking the X in the top right corner of it.

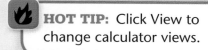 **HOT TIP:** Click View to change calculator views.

 **SEE ALSO:** 'Open an application' in Chapter 2.

Play Solitaire

Windows 7 comes with lots of games. You access the games from the Games folder on the Start menu. Each game offers instructions for how to play it and, for the most part, moving a player, tile or card, dealing a card, or otherwise moving around the screen is performed using the mouse.

1 Click Start.

2 Click Games.

3 Double-click Solitaire to begin the game.

4 Double-click any card to move it to the top piles automatically, or drag a card to move it to the desired location.

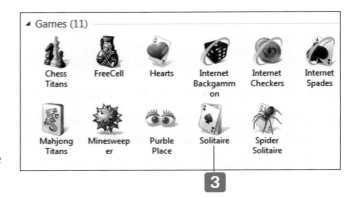

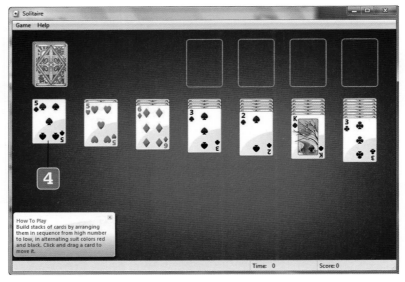

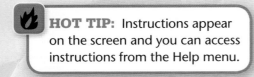

HOT TIP: Instructions appear on the screen and you can access instructions from the Help menu.

Empty the Recycle Bin

The Recycle Bin holds deleted files until you decide to empty it. The Recycle Bin serves as a safeguard, allowing you to recover items accidentally deleted or items you thought you no longer wanted but later decide you need.

1 Locate the Recycle Bin on the desktop and double-click it to open it.

2 Look at the items in the Recycle Bin. If there's something there you want to keep then right-click the item and then click Restore.

3 Click the red X in the top right corner to close the Recycle Bin window.

4 If you're sure you want to empty the Recycle Bin, right-click the Recycle Bin icon on the desktop and click Empty Recycle Bin.

5 When prompted click Yes.

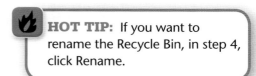

Recycle bin

HOT TIP: If you want to rename the Recycle Bin, in step 4, click Rename.

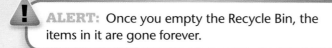

ALERT: Once you empty the Recycle Bin, the items in it are gone forever.

4 Work with files and folders

Introduction

When you use your computer, you often create and obtain data. This data can be letters, pictures, to-do lists, and even music and video you get from the internet. To keep the data on your computer and thus always available, you save it. You save data as a file, and you store files in folders. It's very similar to how you'd store data (documents and pictures) in a physical filing cabinet.

When you choose to save data, you're prompted by Windows 7 to save it in a folder that represents the data you want to save. For instance, when saving a document, you're prompted to save it in the Documents folder, when saving or uploading pictures, you're prompted to save them to the Pictures folder, and so on.

In this chapter you'll learn where files are saved by default, and how to create your own folders and subfolders for organising data. You'll also learn how to copy, move and delete files and folders, how to locate saved files, and how to perform searches for data when you can't find it.

Locate your personal folders

You should save data to your personal folders. In Windows 7, these folders are already created for you and include My Pictures, My Music, My Documents, My Videos, Contacts, Downloads and others.

Note: You'll also see Libraries named Documents, Music, Pictures, Public and Videos. You'll learn more about Libraries next.

1 Click the Start menu and click your user name.

2 Alternatively, click the folder icon on the taskbar.

3 Review the icons in your personal folder.

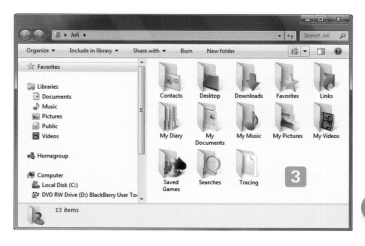

DID YOU KNOW?
You can access some of your personal folders directly from the Start menu, like Documents and Pictures.

HOT TIP: When you're ready to save data, you're going to want to save it to the folder that most closely matches the data you're saving. Documents belong in the My Documents folder and Pictures belong in the My Pictures folder.

WHAT DOES THIS MEAN?

Your personal folder contains the following folders, which in turn contain data you've saved. You'll be most concerned with the following:

Contacts: This folder contains your contacts' information, which includes email addresses, pictures, phone numbers, home and businesses addresses, and more.

Desktop: This folder contains links to items for data you created on your desktop.

Documents: This folder contains documents you've saved and subfolders you've created.

Downloads: This folder does not contain anything by default. Instead it offers a place to save items you download from the internet, like drivers and third-party programs.

Favorites: This folder contains the items in Internet Explorer's Favorites list. It may also include folders created by the computer manufacturer or Microsoft.

My Music: This folder contains music you save to the PC.

My Pictures: This folder contains pictures you save to the PC.

Searches: This folder offers a place to save search folders you create from the results of searches you generate from any search window.

Videos: This folder contains videos you save to the PC.

Explore Libraries

Libraries are different from folders, in that they offer a place to access related data. The Documents Library lets you access documents stored in the My Documents folder, the Public documents folder (detailed next), and any subfolders you've created.

1 Click the folder icon on the taskbar.

2 Click Libraries.

3 Click any Library icon to view its contents.

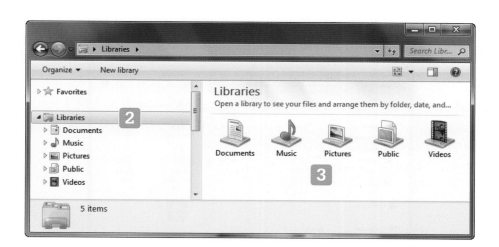

Explore Public folders

Public folders offer a place to store data you want to share with others. When you put data in Public folders, anyone on your home network or anyone that has a user account on your computer can access them. This keeps you from having duplicate data on your home PCs, and reduces clutter.

1 Click Start, and click Computer.

2 Double-click Local Disk (C:); double-click Users; double-click Public. (This is not shown.)

3 Review the folders inside the Public folder.

🔥 **HOT TIP:** Anything you store in your Public folders can be accessed by others on your network if Public Sharing is enabled in the Network and Sharing Center. See Chapter 11.

❓ **DID YOU KNOW?**

You can place a shortcut to the Public folders on your Desktop by right-clicking Public in step 2, and clicking Send To, and Desktop (Create Shortcut).

Create a folder

Your personal folders will suit your needs for a while, but you may want to create folders of your own. You can create a folder on the desktop or inside other folders to hold information you access often.

1 Right-click an empty area of your desktop.

2 Point to New.

3 Click Folder.

4 Type a name for the folder.

5 Press Enter on the keyboard.

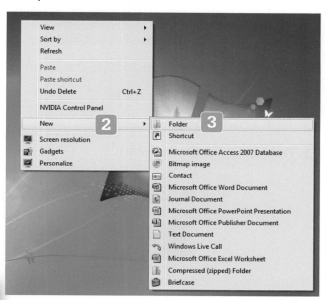

ALERT: If you can't type a name for the folder, right-click the folder and select Rename.

? DID YOU KNOW?
You can drag the folder to another area of the desktop or even to another area of the hard drive to move it there.

🔥 HOT TIP: Create a folder to hold data related to a hobby, tax information, work or family.

Create a subfolder

You can also create folders inside other folders. For instance, inside the My Documents folder, you may want to create a subfolder called Tax Information to hold scanned receipts, tax records and account information. Inside the My Pictures folder you might create folders named 2010, 2011, 2012, or Weddings, Holidays, Grandchildren, and so on.

1 Click the folder icon on the taskbar to open your personal folder.

2 Open the folder that needs a subfolder.

3 Right-click an empty area inside the folder.

4 Point to New and click Folder.

5 Type a name for the folder.

6 Press Enter on the keyboard.

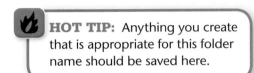

HOT TIP: Anything you create that is appropriate for this folder name should be saved here.

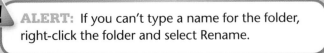

ALERT: If you can't type a name for the folder, right-click the folder and select Rename.

Copy a file

Folders contain files that you save there. Sometimes you'll need to copy a file to another location. Perhaps you want to copy the files to an external drive, memory card or USB thumb drive for the purpose of backing it up, or maybe you want to create a copy so you can edit the data in it without worrying about changing the original.

1 Locate a file to copy.

2 Right-click the file.

3 While holding down the right mouse key, drag the file to the new location. (It's okay if you see 'Move to Desktop' as shown here. You'll get the option to copy when you drop the file.)

4 Drop it there.

5 Choose Copy here.

 ALERT: To copy a file you first have to 'browse' to it. Open your personal folders to find a file to copy.

 HOT TIP: If you don't have any files yet, search for Sample Pictures from the Start menu. Click the Sample Pictures folder and use these files to experiment.

 ALERT: To delete the copy, right click it and choose Delete.

Move a file

When you copy something, an exact duplicate is made. For the most part, this is not what you want to do with data (unless you're backing it up). You generally want to move data. If a picture of a graduation needs to be put in the Graduation Pictures folder, you need to move it, not copy it.

1 Locate a file to move.

2 Right-click the file.

3 While holding down the right mouse key, drag the file to the new location.

4 Drop it there.

5 Choose Move here.

HOT TIP: If you've experimented with the Sample Pictures, to put the file back in its original location, repeat these steps dragging the file from the desktop back to the Sample Pictures folder.

DID YOU KNOW?
You move a file the same way you copy one, except when you drop the file you choose Move here instead of Copy here.

Delete a file

When you are sure you no longer need a particular file, you can delete it. Deleting it sends the file to the Recycle Bin. This file can be 'restored' if you decide you need the file later, provided you have not emptied the Recycle Bin since deleting it.

1 Locate a file to delete.

2 Right-click the file.

3 Choose Delete.

? DID YOU KNOW?

It's best to keep unwanted or unnecessary data off your hard drive. That means you should delete data you don't need, including items in the Recycle Bin.

Copy a folder

Folders often contain other folders (subfolders). Sometimes you'll need to copy a folder to another location. Perhaps you want to copy the folder to an external drive, memory card or USB thumb drive for the purpose of backing it up, or maybe you want to create a copy so you can edit the data in it without worrying about changing the original.

1 Locate a folder to copy.

2 Right-click the folder.

3 While holding down the right mouse key, drag the folder to the new location.

4 Drop it there.

5 Choose Copy here.

ALERT: When you copy a folder, you copy *all* of the data inside it.

HOT TIP: Don't worry that the informative pop-up says 'move'; you'll have the option to copy once you drop the file.

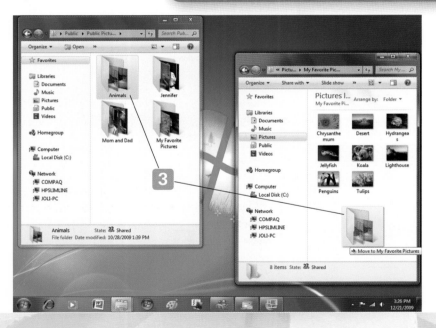

ALERT: To delete the copy, right-click it and choose Delete.

DID YOU KNOW?
When you delete a copy of a folder, the original folder remains intact.

Move a folder

If you created a folder on your desktop, you may want to move the folder (and all its contents) to the inside of one of your personal folders. You may also want to move folders for the purpose of organising them.

1 Locate a folder to move.

2 Open the folder you want to move it to. (For instance, open your personal folder by clicking your name on the Start menu.)

3 Right-click the folder you want to move.

4 While holding down the right mouse key, drag the folder to the new location. You can drag a folder onto the top of the receiving folder, as shown here, if desired.

5 Drop it there, noting that you've selected the proper folder, shown here.

6 Choose Move here.

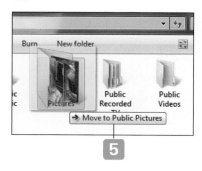

? **DID YOU KNOW?**

Keeping all of your data in your personal folders will help keep your desktop uncluttered, but it also makes backing up the data later easier (because all of your data is in one place and because the data can be categorised into appropriate Libraries).

? **DID YOU KNOW?**

You may have to open a folder to locate the folder you want to move.

Delete a folder

When you are sure you no longer need a particular folder, you can delete it. When you delete a folder you delete the folder and everything in it. Deleting it sends the folder and its contents to the Recycle Bin. This folder can be 'restored' if you decide you need it later, provided you have not emptied the Recycle Bin since deleting it.

1 Locate a folder to delete.

2 Right-click the folder.

3 Choose Delete.

? DID YOU KNOW?

It's best to keep unwanted or unnecessary data off your hard drive. That means you should delete data you don't need, including items in the Recycle Bin.

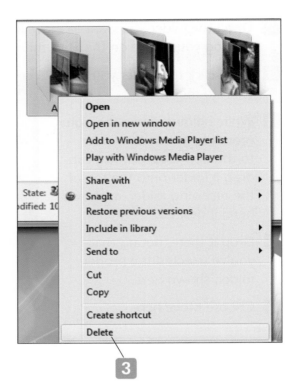

Open a saved file

Once data (in this case, a file) is saved to your hard drive, you can access it, open it and often modify it. Most of the time, you open a saved file from a personal folder or a folder you've created.

1 Click Start.

2 Click Documents.

3 Locate the file to open in the Documents folder.

4 Double-click it to open it.

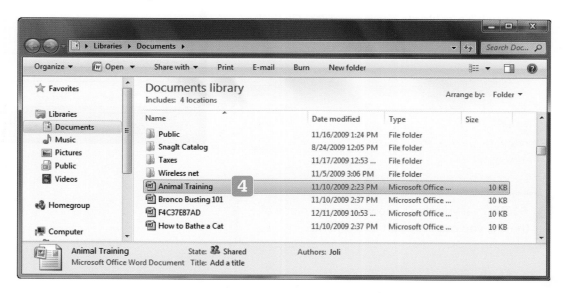

? **DID YOU KNOW?**

The file will open in the appropriate program automatically.

▶ **SEE ALSO:** 'Write a letter with Notepad' and 'Save a letter with Notepad' in Chapter 3 to learn how to create and save a text file.

Search for a lost file

After you create data, like a document, you save it to your hard drive. When you're ready to use the file again, you have to locate it and open it. If you know the document is in the Documents folder, you can click Start, and then click Documents. Then, you can simply double-click the file to open it. However, if you aren't sure where the file is, you'll have to search for it.

1 Click Start.

2 In the Start Search window, type the name of the file.

3 There will be multiple search results. Click the file to open it.

ALERT: If you don't know the exact name of the file, you can type part of the name.

? DID YOU KNOW?
If you don't know any part of the name of the file, you can type a word that is included inside the file.

Back up a folder (or file) to an external drive

Once you have your data saved in folders, you can copy both files and folders to an external drive to create a backup. You'll copy the data to the external drive using the drag and drop technique you learned earlier in this chapter. However, before you begin, plug in and/or attach the external drive.

1 Click Start and click Computer.

2 Locate the external drive. (Leave this window open and resize it so that it takes up only part of the screen.)

3 Locate the data to copy. Resize the window so you can drag the data to the external drive.

4 Right-click the file or folder to copy.

5 While holding down the right mouse key, drag the folder to the new location.

6 Drop it there and choose Copy here.

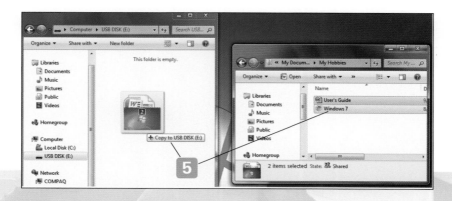

 **ALERT:** Don't choose Move here. This will move the folder off the computer and onto the hard drive.

SEE ALSO: 'Resize a window', in Chapter 5.

5 Work with windows

Introduction

So far you've learned quite a bit about your computer and how to use it. What you haven't learned is how to work with windows. The term *windows*, as it is used in this chapter, is not capitalised and does not have anything to do with any product name (for instance, Microsoft Windows 7 or Windows Live Essentials). Here, the term windows is used to represent a part of the interface that you will use to access files inside a folder *window*, menus inside an application *window*, and settings available in the Control Panel *window*.

To work with windows requires you to know how to resize, move or arrange these open windows on your desktop. This is essential because each time you open a program, file, folder, picture or anything else, a new window almost always opens. You have to be very familiar with these windows, including how to show or hide them, in order to become comfortable navigating your computer.

Change the view in a window

When you open your personal folder from the Start menu or from the taskbar, you will see additional folders inside it. You open any of these subfolders to see what's inside them. You can change what the content inside these folders looks like by changing how large or small their icons appear. You can configure each folder independently so that the data appears in a list, as small icons or as large icons, to name a few.

1 Click Start.

2 Click Pictures.

3 Click the arrow next to the Change your view button.

4 Move the slider to select an option from the list.

 HOT TIP: Show items in the Pictures folder as large or extra large icons, and you'll be able to tell what each picture looks like without actually opening it in a program.

 HOT TIP: Show items in the Documents window as Details to see the name of each document as well as the date it was created.

Minimise a window

When you have several open windows, you may want to minimise (hide) the windows you aren't using. A minimised window appears on the taskbar as a small icon, and is not on the desktop. When you're ready to use the window again, you simply click it.

1 Open any window. (Click Start, and then click Pictures, Documents, Games or any other option.)

2 Click the – sign in the top right corner.

3 Locate the window title in the taskbar. Position your mouse over the icon to see its thumbnail.

WHAT DOES THIS MEAN?

Taskbar: the transparent bar that runs across the bottom of your screen. It contains the Start button and the Notification area.

 ALERT: A minimised window is on the taskbar, and is not shown on the desktop. You can 'restore' the window by clicking on its icon on the taskbar. Restoring a window to the desktop brings the window back up so you can work with it.

Minimise multiple windows

Sometimes you'll have lots of windows open and you want to minimise all of them simultaneously, except for the one you want to work with. You can do this by *shaking* the window you want to keep, which causes the other open windows to fall to the taskbar.

1 Open multiple windows, including Documents, Pictures, Computer and others.

2 Click the windows you'd like to keep on the desktop with the left mouse button, hold down that button, and quickly move the mouse left and right.

3 Repeat step 2 to restore the windows to the desktop.

DID YOU KNOW?
Shake and Peek are new to Windows 7.

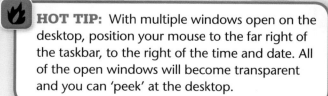
HOT TIP: With multiple windows open on the desktop, position your mouse to the far right of the taskbar, to the right of the time and date. All of the open windows will become transparent and you can 'peek' at the desktop.

Restore a window

A window can be minimised (on the taskbar), maximised (filling the entire desktop), or be in restore mode (not maximised or minimised, but showing on the desktop). A maximised window has two small squares in the top right corner and takes up the entire screen; a window in restore mode only has one square in the top right corner and does not fill the entire screen.

1 Open a window.

2 If the window is not taking up the entire screen, click the top of the window with your mouse and drag it upwards. It will maximise.

3 To put the window in restore mode, click the top of the (maximised) window with your mouse and drag downward.

click and drag here

ALERT: Remember, if you don't see two squares but instead only see one, the window is already in restore mode.

HOT TIP: If the window has been minimised to the taskbar, click it to bring it to the desktop, then maximise or restore it.

Restore multiple windows

Shake, detailed in the 'Minimise multiple windows' section, allows you to minimise all open windows except the one you want by clicking and shaking the top of the window. You can click and shake the top of a single open window to restore the others.

1 Open multiple windows.

2 Click any window on the desktop with the left mouse button, hold down that button, and quickly move the mouse left and right. This minimises the windows.

3 Repeat step 2 to restore the windows to the desktop.

? DID YOU KNOW?
You can drag any window to the left or right side of the screen to automatically resize it to take up exactly half of the screen. This is called 'Snap'.

🔥 HOT TIP: If you're working on a computer with limited resources, close open windows you aren't using for better performance.

Maximise a window

A maximised window is as large as it can be, and takes up the entire screen. You can maximise a window that is on the desktop by clicking the square icon in the top right corner. If the icon is already a square, it's already maximized. You can also drag the window to the top of the screen, as detailed earlier.

1 Open a window.

2 In the top right corner of the window, locate the square.

3 Click it to maximise the window.

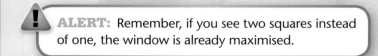

ALERT: Remember, if you see two squares instead of one, the window is already maximised.

Move a window

You can move a window as long as it's in restore mode. You move a window by dragging it from its title bar. The title bar is the bar that runs across the top of the window. Moving windows allows you to position multiple windows across the screen.

1 Open any window.

2 Put the window in restore mode if it is not already.

3 Left-click with the mouse on the top of the window and drag. Let go of the mouse when the window is positioned correctly.

click and drag here

Resize a window

Resizing a window allows you to change the dimensions of the window. You can resize a window by dragging from its sides, corners or the top and bottom.

1 Open any window. (If you're unsure, click Start and Pictures.)

2 Put the window in restore mode. You want the maximise button to show.

3 Position the mouse at one of the window corners, so that the mouse pointer becomes a two-pointed arrow.

4 Hold down the mouse button and drag the arrow to resize the window.

5 Repeat as desired, dragging from the sides, top, bottom or corners.

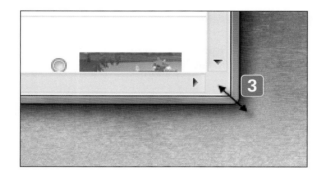

 ALERT: You can only resize windows in this manner if they are in 'restore' mode, meaning the maximise button is showing in the top right corner of the window.

Reposition a window to take up half the screen

Sometimes you need to reposition windows so they take up half the screen, especially when you want to drag files from one location to another to move or copy them. You can position windows easily with a feature called Snap.

1 Click Start, and click Pictures.

2 Drag the folder from its titlebar to the right side of the screen.

3 Click Start, and click Computer.

4 Drag the Computer window using its titlebar to the left side of the screen.

? DID YOU KNOW?

You can position these two windows to drag files from your Pictures folder to a connected USB drive to back up your data.

► SEE ALSO: Learn more about copying and moving files in Chapter 4.

6 Personalise Windows 7

Introduction

You can personalise Windows 7 to suit your tastes and needs. There are lots of desktop backgrounds and the option to rotate backgrounds automatically and on a schedule, for instance. You can add a screen saver. You can add your favourite system icons to the desktop as well as shortcuts to programs you use often. You can also change the properties of the taskbar, and pin applications there for easy access. You can even add 'gadgets' to your desktop that offer information about the time, weather, news and more.

Change the desktop background

If you have yet to personalise the picture on your desktop, now's the time to do that. That picture is called the background.

1 Right-click an empty area of the desktop.

2 Click Personalize.

3 Click Desktop Background.

4 For Location, select Windows Desktop Backgrounds. If it is not chosen already, click the down arrow to locate it.

5 Use the scroll bars to locate the wallpaper to use as your desktop background.

6 Select a background to use or select multiple backgrounds as shown here.

7 Select a positioning option (the default, Fill, is the most common).

8 Select how often to change the backgrounds, if you selected more than one.

9 Click Save changes.

10 Click the red X in the top right corner of the Personalization window to close it.

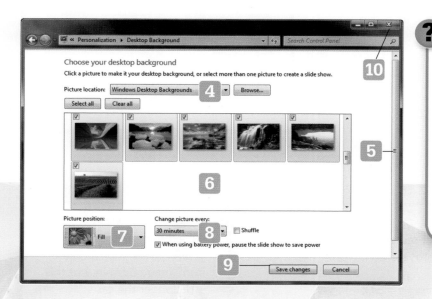

? DID YOU KNOW?

You can click the Browse button to locate a picture you've taken, acquired or otherwise saved to your computer, and use it for a desktop background. Pictures are usually found in the Pictures folder.

Change the screen saver

A screen saver is a picture or animation that covers your screen and appears after your computer has been idle for a specific amount of time that you set. Screen savers are used for either visual enhancement or as a security feature. For security, you can configure your screen saver to require a password on waking up, which happens when you move the mouse or hit a key on the keyboard. Requiring a password means that once the screen saver is running, no one can log onto your computer but you, by typing in your password when prompted.

1 Right-click an empty area of the desktop.

2 Click Personalize.

3 Click Screen Saver.

Screen Saver
None

4 Click the arrow to see the available screen savers and select one.

5 Use the arrows to change how long to wait before the screen saver is enabled.

6 If desired, click On resume, display logon screen to require a password to log back into the computer.

7 Click OK.

Add desktop icons

When Windows 7 started the first time, it may have had only one item on the desktop, the Recycle Bin. Alternatively, it may have had 20 or more. What appears on your desktop the first time Windows boots up depends on a number of factors, including who manufactured your computer.

1 Right-click an empty area of the desktop.

2 Click Personalize.

3 Click Change desktop icons.

4 Select the desktop icons you want to appear on your desktop.

5 Click OK.

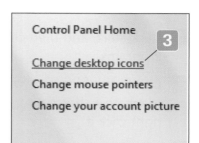

HOT TIP: You can remove desktop icons by deselecting them here.

WHAT DOES THIS MEAN?

Icon: A visual representation of an application, feature or program.

Create a shortcut on the desktop

Shortcuts you place on the desktop let you access folders, files, programs and other items by double-clicking them. Shortcuts always appear with an arrow beside them (or on them, actually). The easiest way to create a shortcut to a program (or other item) you access often is to locate it and right-click it. To create a shortcut for a program installed on your computer, you'll have to find it in the All Programs menu, as detailed here.

1 Click Start, and then click All Programs.

2 Locate the program you'd like to create a shortcut for and right-click it.

3 Click Send to.

4 Click Desktop (create shortcut).

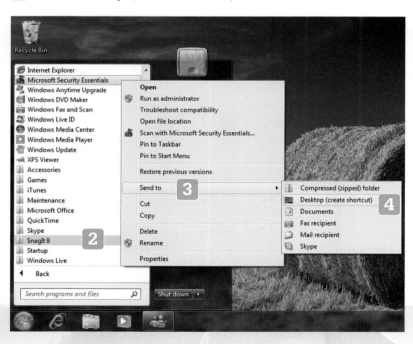

HOT TIP: You can create a shortcut for a file, folder, picture, song or other item by locating it and right-clicking, as detailed in this section.

 ALERT: You can delete a shortcut by dragging it to the Recycle Bin. Be careful though; only delete shortcuts – don't delete any actual folders!

Search for anything from the Start menu

To locate a program, file, folder, song, picture or anything else stored on your computer, type a little about it in Start Search window. Just type in what you're looking for, and select the appropriate item from the list. Note that when you search using the Start Search window, all kinds of results will appear, including email, applications, documents and pictures.

1 Click Start.

2 In the Start Search window, type Media.

3 Note the results.

4 Click any result to open it. If you want to open Windows Media Center, click it once. Note that it's under Programs.

HOT TIP: The easiest way to find something on your computer is to type it into this search window.

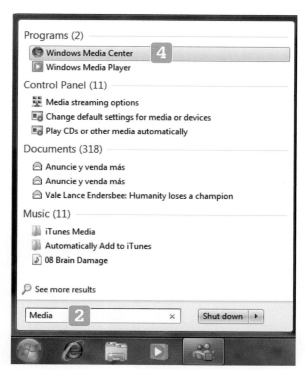

Add a gadget to the desktop

Gadgets sit on your desktop and offer information about the weather, time and date, as well as access to your contacts, productivity tools and CPU usage. You can even have a slideshow of your favourite pictures. You can customise your desktop by adding gadgets and customising these to meet your needs.

1 In the Start Search window, type Gadgets.

2 Under Programs, click Desktop Gadget Gallery.

3 Drag any gadget to the desktop. You can drag as many as you like.

4 Click the X in the top right corner of the Desktop Gadget Gallery to close it.

HOT TIP: Drag the clock and weather gadgets to the desktop.

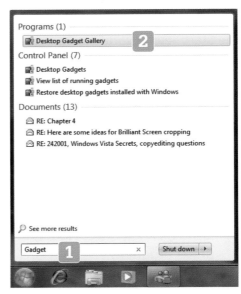

Programs (1)
Desktop Gadget Gallery

Control Panel (7)
Desktop Gadgets
View list of running gadgets
Restore desktop gadgets installed with Windows

Documents (13)
RE: Chapter 4
RE: Here are some ideas for Brilliant Screen cropping
RE: 242001, Windows Vista Secrets, copyediting questions

See more results

Gadget

Shut down

Page 1 of 2   Search gadgets

Some gadgets access the Internet. For more information, see the privacy statement online.

Calendar   Clock   CPU Meter   Currency

Feed Headlines   Picture Puzzle   Slide Show   Weather

Show details

ALERT: You won't get up-to-date information on the weather, stocks and other real-time gadgets unless you're connected to the internet.

Set the time on the clock gadget

Almost all gadgets offer a wrench icon when you position your cursor over them. You can use this icon to access settings for the gadget. The first thing you may want to configure is the clock gadget.

1 Position the cursor over the clock you dragged to the desktop. Look for the small x and the wrench to appear. Click the wrench icon.

2 Click the arrow in the Time zone window and select your time zone from the list.

3 Click the right arrow underneath the clock to change the clock type. Type a clock name if you like.

4 Click the left and right arrows to select a new clock, if desired.

5 Click OK.

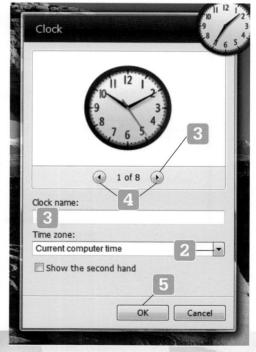

DID YOU KNOW?
Clicking the x will remove the gadget from the desktop. Clicking the wrench will open the gadget's properties, if properties are available.

ALERT: The Stocks gadget runs about 15 minutes behind real-time stock data, so don't start buying and selling based on what you see here!

Configure the taskbar

The taskbar has a new look. It is transparent and blends in nicely with the desktop. You can configure the taskbar by right-clicking and choosing Properties, and you can lock or hide the taskbar using the options on the Properties page.

1 Right-click the taskbar and click Properties.

2 Make changes as desired.

3 Click OK.

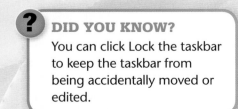

? DID YOU KNOW?
You can click Lock the taskbar to keep the taskbar from being accidentally moved or edited.

HOT TIP: Click the Start Menu and Toolbars tabs to make changes as desired.

HOT TIP: Hide the taskbar for more screen 'real estate'.

Pin icons to the taskbar

If there's a program you use often, consider pinning it to the taskbar. That way, you can access it with a single click of the mouse.

1 Locate the program you want to pin to the taskbar in the Start menu (or the All Programs menu).

2 Right-click it and choose Pin to Taskbar.

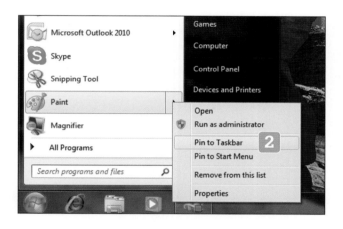

? **DID YOU KNOW?**

From this same area you can pin an icon to the Start menu or remove an item from the Start Menu or All Programs list.

7 Surf the internet

Introduction

Your computer came with a 'web browser', a program that allows you to surf the internet. The name of the web browser installed on your computer is Internet Explorer. Internet Explorer allows you to open websites, keep multiple webpages open at the same time, configure Home pages, mark Favorites, and more.

You can open Internet Explorer in a number of ways, but the easiest is from the taskbar that runs across the bottom of your computer screen. Once open, you can type 'keywords' to search for information you want, go directly to websites by typing their name into the address bar, or choose from a list of bookmarks included with Internet Explorer or from those you've saved yourself.

Open a website in Internet Explorer

Windows 7 comes with Internet Explorer, an application you can use to surf the internet. The first step in web surfing is to open Internet Explorer and then a webpage.

1 Open Internet Explorer from the taskbar. It's a big, blue E. A website will probably open automatically.

2 To go to a website you want to visit, type the name of the website in the window at the top of the page. This is called the address bar.

3 Press Enter on the keyboard.

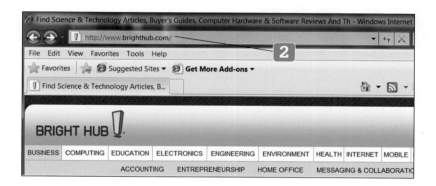

 HOT TIP: You can also drag your mouse across an open website name to select it. Do not drag your mouse over the http://www part of the address or you'll just have to retype it.

HOT TIP: Every webpage contains a link to another webpage. Click the links to move from one page to another on the internet.

ALERT: Websites almost always start with http://www.

Open a website in a new tab

You can open more than one website at a time in Internet Explorer. To do this, click the tab that appears to the right of the open webpage. Then, type the name of the website you'd like to visit.

1 Open Internet Explorer.

2 Click an empty tab.

3 Type the name of the website you'd like to visit in the address bar.

4 Press Enter on the keyboard.

HOT TIP: Type the following:
http://www.microsoft.com/uk

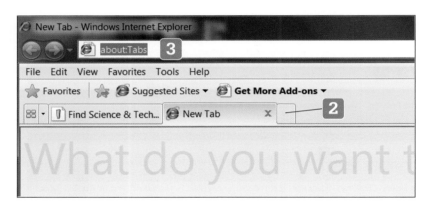

? DID YOU KNOW?

When a website name starts with https://, it means it's secure. When purchasing items online, make sure the payment pages have this prefix.

WHAT DOES THIS MEAN?

The Internet Explorer interface has several distinct parts.

Command bar: Used to access icons such as the Home and Print icons.

Tabs: Used to access websites when multiple sites are open.

Search window: Used to search for anything on the internet.

Set a home page

You can select a single webpage or multiple webpages to be displayed each time you open Internet Explorer. In fact, there are three options for configuring home pages:

- Use this webpage as your only home page: Select this option if you only want one page to serve as your home page.

- Add this webpage to your home page tabs: Select this option if you want this page to be one of several home pages.

- Use the current tab set as your home page: Select this option if you've opened multiple tabs and you want all of them to be home pages.

1 Use the Address bar to locate a webpage you want to use as your home page.

2 Click the arrow next to the Home icon.

3 Click Add or Change Home Page.

4 Make a selection using the information provided regarding each option. If you've never set a home page before, you'll need to select Use this webpage as your only home page.

5 Click Yes.

6 Repeat these steps as desired.

SEE ALSO: 'Open a website in Internet Explorer', earlier in this chapter.

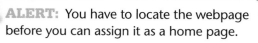

ALERT: You have to locate the webpage before you can assign it as a home page.

HOT TIP: To open your home pages, click the Home icon on the toolbar.

Mark a favourite

Favourites are websites you save links to for accessing more easily at a later time. They differ from home pages because, by default, they do not open when you start Internet Explorer. The favourites you save appear in the Favorites Center and on the Favorites bar. You may see some favourites listed that you did not create, including Microsoft websites and MSN websites. Every time you save a favourite, it will appear in both places.

1 Go to the webpage you want to configure as a favourite.

2 Click the Add to Favorites icon.

3 Note the new icon for the favourite on the Favorites bar.

4 Click the Favorites icon. The Favorites Center opens.

5 Click the folders to view the favourites listed in them.

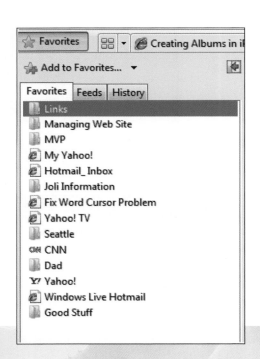

HOT TIP: You can organise your favourites in your personal Favorites folder.

Change the zoom level of a webpage

If you have trouble reading what's on a webpage because the text is too small, use the Page Zoom feature. Page Zoom works by preserving the fundamental design of the webpage you're viewing. This means that Page Zoom intelligently zooms in on the entire page, which maintains the page's integrity, layout and look.

1 Open Internet Explorer and browse to a webpage.

2 Click the arrow located at the bottom right of Internet Explorer to show the Zoom options.

3 Click 150%.

4 Notice how the webpage text and images increase. Use the scroll bars to navigate the page.

? **DID YOU KNOW?**

The term 'browse' is used both to describe locating a file on your hard drive and locating something on the internet.

? **DID YOU KNOW?**

The Page Zoom options are located under the Page icon on the command bar, under Zoom, but it's much easier to use the link at the bottom right of the browser window, on the status bar.

Print a webpage

To print a webpage, simply click the Print icon on the command bar.

1 Open Internet Explorer and browse to a webpage.

2 Click the Print icon to print the page with no further input. To view print options, click the arrow next to the Print icon, as shown here.

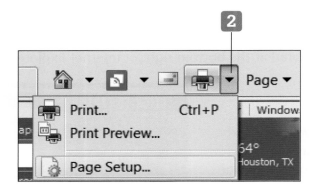

WHAT DOES THIS MEAN?

There are three menu options under the Print icon:

Print: Clicking Print opens the Print dialogue box where you can configure the page range, select a printer, change page orientation, change print order and choose a paper type. Additional options include print quality, output bins, and more. Of course, the choices offered depend on what your printer offers. If your printer can only print at 300 x 300 dots per inch, you can't configure it to print at a higher quality.

Print Preview: Clicking Print Preview opens a window where you can see before you print what the printout will actually look like. You can switch between portrait and landscape views, access the Page Setup dialogue box, and more.

Page Setup: Clicking Page Setup opens the Page Setup dialogue box. Here you can select a paper size, paper source, and create headers and footers. You can also change orientation and margins, all of which is dependent on what features your printer supports.

Clear history

If you don't want people to be able to snoop around on your computer and find out what sites you've been visiting you'll need to delete your 'browsing history'. Deleting your browsing history lets you remove the information stored on your computer related to your internet activities.

1 Open Internet Explorer.

2 Click Safety.

3 Click Delete Browsing History.

4 To delete any or all of the listed items, click the Delete button.

5 Click Close when finished.

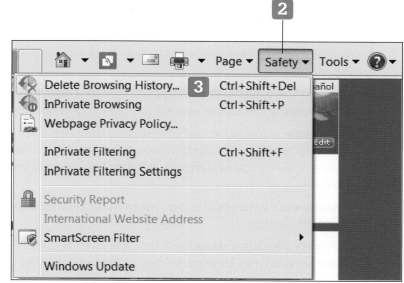

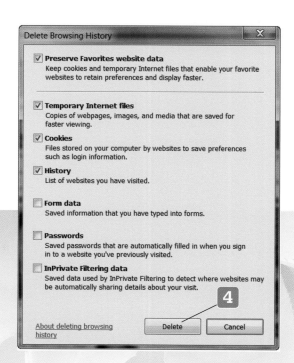

WHAT DOES THIS MEAN?

Temporary Internet Files: These are files that have been downloaded and saved in your Temporary Internet Files folder. A snooper could go through these files to see what you've been doing online.

Cookies: These are small text files that include data that identifies your preferences when you visit particular websites. Cookies allow you to visit, say, www.amazon.com and be greeted with 'Hello <your name>, We have recommendations for you!' Cookies help a site offer you a personalised web experience.

History: This is the list of websites you've visited and any web addresses you've typed. Anyone can look at your History list to see where you've been.

Form data: Information that's been saved using the Internet Explorer's autocomplete form data functionality. If you don't want forms to be filled out automatically by you or someone else who has access to your PC and user account, delete this.

Passwords: Passwords that were saved using Internet Explorer autocomplete password prompts.

InPrivate Blocking data: Data that was saved by InPrivate Blocking to detect where websites may be automatically sharing details about your visit.

Stay safe online

There's a chapter in this book on security, Chapter 13. In it, you'll learn how to use Windows Firewall, Windows Defender and other Security Center features. However, much of staying secure when online and surfing the internet has more to do with common sense. When you're online, make sure to follow the guidelines listed next.

1 If you are connecting to a public network, make sure you select Public when prompted by Windows 7.

2 Always keep your PCs secure with anti-virus software.

3 Limit the amount of confidential information you store on the internet.

4 When making credit card purchases or travel reservations, always make sure the website address starts with https://.

5 Always sign out (log out) of any secure website you enter.

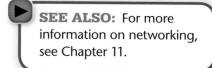

SEE ALSO: For more information on networking, see Chapter 11.

? DID YOU KNOW?
When you connect to a network you know, like a network in your home, you select Home (or Work).

! ALERT: You have to purchase and install your own anti-virus software; it does not come with Windows 7.

! ALERT: Don't put your address and phone number on Facebook or other social networking sites.

WHAT DOES THIS MEAN?

Domain Name: For our use here, a domain name is synonymous with a website name.

Favorite: A webpage that you've chosen to maintain a shortcut for in the Favorites Center.

Home page: The webpage that opens when you open Internet Explorer. You can set the home page and configure additional pages to open as well.

Link: A shortcut to a webpage. Links are often offered in an email, document or webpage to allow you to access a site without having to actually type in its name. In almost all instances, links are underlined and in a different colour than the page they are configured on.

Load: A webpage must 'load' before you can access it. Some pages load instantly while others take a few seconds.

Navigate: The process of moving from one webpage to another or viewing items on a single webpage. Often the term is used as follows 'Click the link to navigate to the new Web page'.

Search: A term used when you type a word or group of words into a Search window. Searching for data produces results.

Scroll Up and Scroll Down: A process of using the scroll bars on a webpage or the arrow keys on a keyboard to move up and down the pages of a website.

Website: A group of webpages that contain related information. Microsoft's website contains information about Microsoft products, for instance.

URL: The information you type to access a website, like http://www.microsoft.com.

8 Get Windows Live Essentials

Introduction

Windows 7 doesn't come with an email program, a messaging program or a photo-editing program. Windows Vista and Windows XP both did, but not Windows 7. You'll need to choose the programs you want to replace these, and we suggest Windows Live Essentials. Once you've installed Live Essentials, obtained an ID and signed in, you'll also have access to a personalised webpage you can customise.

Windows Live Essentials contains all the programs you'll need to manage email, instant message with contacts, edit photos and even create and edit your own movies. You can choose to install additional applications from the suite too, including the Internet Explorer toolbar that connects all of this together seamlessly.

Download and install Windows Live Essentials

If you've never downloaded and/or installed a program before, you may be a little nervous about doing so. Don't worry, it's really easy, and Microsoft has set it up so that the process requires very little input from you. There are only a few steps: go to the website, click the Download link, and wait for the download and installation process to complete.

1 Open Internet Explorer and go to http://download.live.com/.

2 Look for the Download button and click it. You'll be prompted to click Download once more on the next screen.

3 Click Run, and when prompted, click Yes.

4 When prompted, select the items to download. You can select all of the items or only some of them. (Make sure you select Live Mail and Live Photo Gallery at least.)

5 Click Install.

6 When prompted to select your settings, make the desired choices. You can't go wrong here; there are no bad options.

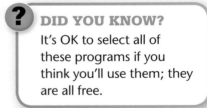

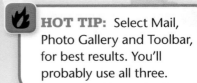

DID YOU KNOW?
It's OK to select all of these programs if you think you'll use them; they are all free.

HOT TIP: Select Mail, Photo Gallery and Toolbar, for best results. You'll probably use all three.

Get a Windows Live ID

When you use 'Live' services, like Windows Live Mail, Windows Live Photo Gallery and others, you have to log in to them using a Windows Live account. This account is free, and you can use it to sign in to Live-related websites on the internet. A Windows Live account is an e-mail address and password you use to log on to your Live programs.

1 If you do not already have a Windows Live account, click Sign up after the installation of Live Mail completes. (You can also go to http://signup.live.com.)

2 Fill out the required information and click I accept when finished.

? DID YOU KNOW?
You can use your Windows Live email account as a regular email address, or simply use it to log into Live services on the internet.

🔥 HOT TIP: Fill out the information with true information. This is an ID, after all.

Sign in

Once you've obtained your Windows Live ID, you can log into Live services like Windows Live Mail and Windows Live Photo Gallery. But what's even better than that is that you now have a personalised webpage on the Internet.

1 Open Internet Explorer and navigate to http://login.live.com.

2 Type your new Live ID and password and click Sign in.

3 Click Home.

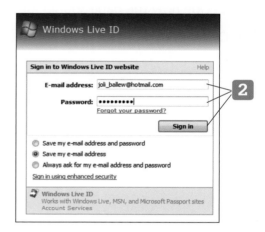

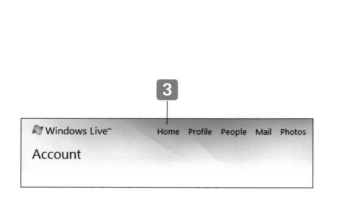

Personalise your Windows Live Home Page

Along with the free Live programs, you'll also get a personalised webpage. You can configure the options on the page to suit your needs. For instance, if you input your postcode you'll get personalised weather information.

1 Log into your new Windows Live Home page, as detailed in the previous section.

2 Click Options, and click Customize this page.

3 Input the desired data, including your postcode.

4 Decide how the page should look.

5 Click Save.

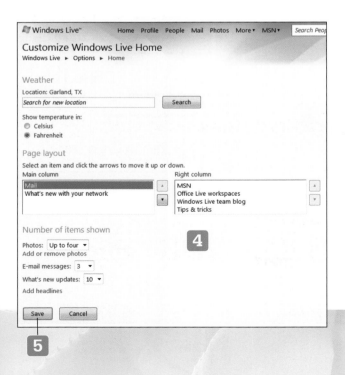

HOT TIP: Click Photos at the top of the page to create an album and upload your favourite photos!

HOT TIP: If you want to use your Live email address, you can get your email right from your Home page. You can also add contacts, share photos, and view private messages from people you know.

Open Windows Live Photo Gallery

In the next chapter you'll learn all about Windows Live Mail. For now though, open Windows Live Photo Gallery to get a glimpse of what you have to look forward to! Live Photo Gallery will help you manage, edit and store your digital photos.

1 Click Start, click All Programs.

2 Click Windows Live, and then click Windows Live Photo Gallery.

3 When prompted, log in with your new Windows Live ID.

4 To view the sample pictures that come with Windows 7, click Sample Pictures in the left pane.

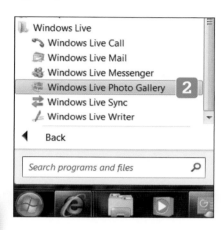

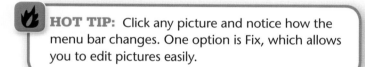

HOT TIP: Click any picture and notice how the menu bar changes. One option is Fix, which allows you to edit pictures easily.

9 Windows Live Mail

Introduction

You want to send and receive email. Your Internet Service Provider (ISP) probably offers a website for doing this. For instance, if your email address is yourname@verizon.net, you can go to http://www.verizon.net, log in and retrieve and send email directly from the Web. However, these 'web-based' email options don't offer very many perks, and it's hard to handle the email you want to keep, work with attachments, send email that contains stationery and pictures, manage contacts, and perform other email-related tasks. It's best to use a program that's installed on your PC versus one that's only available via the Web.

Previous versions of Windows operating systems, like Windows XP and Windows Vista, came with an email program already built-in, and you may be somewhat familiar with them (Outlook Express, Windows Mail). That's not the case with Windows 7. However, Microsoft does offer Windows Live Mail, which you can download and install for free on your Windows 7 PC. Windows Live Mail also lets you access your email from any PC that has internet access, not just the PC in your home or office, so you can have the best of both worlds.

What is Windows Live Mail?

Windows Live Mail is a full-fledged email program that allows you to view, send and receive email, manage your contacts, and manage sent, saved and incoming email. Within Windows Live Mail you can also print email, create folders for storing email you want to keep, manage unwanted email, open attachments, send pictures inside an email, add stationery, and more.

To use Windows Live Mail you'll need to complete some of the tasks already outlined in this book, including downloading and installing Windows Live Essentials (Chapter 8). You'll also need some form of personal internet access like an always-on internet subscription such as cable or DSL, access to a free wireless hotspot, or another option, like wireless or dial-up. If you obtained your email address from a provider like British Telecom, BSkyB, Tesco and the like, you'll also need to gather any personalised email information given to you from your ISP, like server names, your email address and password.

Set up a Windows Live email account

The first time you open Windows Live Mail you'll be prompted to input the required information regarding your email address, password and email servers. That's because Windows Live Mail is a program for sending and receiving email, and you can't do that without inputting the proper information. The easiest email account to set up is your new Windows Live Account, the account you created in Chapter 8.

1 Open Windows Live Mail. (To open Windows Live Mail, click Start, and in the Start Search window, type Live Mail. Click Windows Live Mail in the results.)

2 Click Add an E-mail Account.

3 Type your Windows Live email address, password and display name.

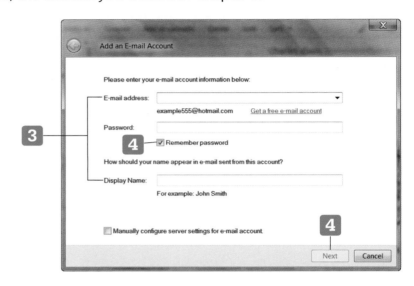

4 If desired, leave Remember password ticked. Click Next.

5 Click Finish and, if prompted, click Download Now to retrieve your email. (Don't tick Manually configure server settings for e-mail account.)

? DID YOU KNOW?

Your email address often takes this form: *yourname@ Live.com*. Your display name can be anything you like.

? DID YOU KNOW?

Your display name is the name that will appear in the From field when you compose an email, and in the sender's Inbox (under From in their email list) when the sender receives email from you.

Set up a third-party email account

When you set up a Windows Live email account, Windows Live knows what settings to use and configure in the background. If you want to set up a third-party email account, you have to enter the settings manually. You get the information you need from your ISP.

1 Open Windows Live Mail, and click Add an E-mail Account as detailed in the previous section.

2 Input your email address, password and display name.

3 When prompted, fill in the information for your incoming and outgoing mail servers. Click Next.

4 Click Finish.

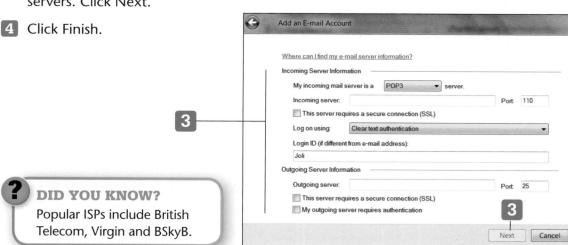

> **? DID YOU KNOW?**
> Popular ISPs include British Telecom, Virgin and BSkyB.

> **⚠ ALERT:** You must input exactly what your ISP tells you to input! When in doubt, call the ISP or check its website for the proper settings.

> **⚠ ALERT:** If your ISP tells you your outgoing server requires authentication, tick the box. If you aren't sure, don't tick it.

> **⚠ ALERT:** To resolve errors, click Tools, click Accounts, click the email account to change, and click Properties. You can then make changes to the mail servers, passwords and other settings.

View an email

Windows Live Mail checks for email automatically when you first open the program and every 30 minutes thereafter. If you want to check for email manually, you can click the Sync button any time you want. When you receive mail, there are two ways to read it. You can click the message one time and read it in the Mail window, or double-click it to open it in its own window. We think it's best to simply click the email one time, that way you don't have multiple open windows to deal with.

1 Click the Sync button.

2 Click the email once.

3 View the contents of the email.

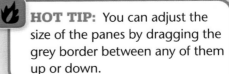

WHAT DOES THIS MEAN?

Inbox: This folder holds mail you've received.

Outbox: This folder holds mail you've written but have not yet sent.

Sent Items: This folder stores copies of messages you've sent.

Deleted Items: This folder holds mail you've deleted.

Drafts: This folder holds messages you've started and saved, but not completed. Click File and click Save to put an email in progress here.

Junk e-mail: This folder holds email that Windows Live Mail thinks is spam. You should check this folder occasionally, because Mail may put email in there you want to read.

Unread e-mail: This folder shows email you have yet to read. Note there is one that contains email from contacts too. The latter only shows email from contacts in your address book.

Change how often Windows Live Mail checks for email

You may want to have Windows Live Mail check for email more or less often than every 30 minutes. It's easy to make the change.

1 Click the Menus icon.

2 Click Options.

3 On the General tab, under Send/Receive Messages, change the number of minutes from 30 to something else.

4 Click OK.

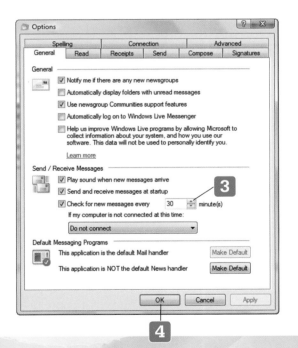

View an attachment

An attachment is a file that you can send with an email like a picture, document, video clip or something similar. If an email you receive contains an attachment, you'll see a paperclip. To open the attachment, click the attachment's name.

1 Locate the paperclip icon in the Message pane. Note the name of the attachment(s).

2 If the attachment is something you are expecting and you know the sender, double-click the attachment name.

3 Click Open.

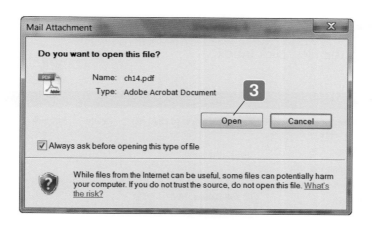

ALERT: Hackers send attachments that look like they are from legitimate companies, banks and online services. Do not open these. Companies rarely send email attachments.

ALERT: Attachments can contain viruses. Never open an attachment from someone you don't know, or one that ends in .zip unless you know the sender.

Recover email from the Junk email folder

Windows Live Mail has a junk email filter and anything it thinks is spam gets sent there. ('Spam' is another word for junk email.) Unfortunately, sometimes email gets sent to the Junk e-mail folder that is actually legitimate email. Therefore, once a week or so you should look in this folder to see if any email you want to keep is in there.

1 Click the Junk email folder one time.

2 Use the scroll bars if necessary to browse through the email in the folder.

3 If you see an email that is legitimate, click it one time.

4 Click Not junk.

5 After reviewing the files, click Inbox.

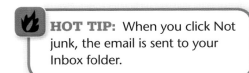

HOT TIP: When you click Not junk, the email is sent to your Inbox folder.

ALERT: Mail requires routine maintenance including deleting email from the Junk e-mail folder, among other things. You'll learn how to delete items in a folder later in this chapter.

HOT TIP: When you tell Mail that a certain email is 'not junk', it remembers and should not flag email from this sender as spam again.

Reply to an email

When someone sends you an email, you may need to send a reply back to them. You do that by selecting the email and then clicking the Reply button.

1 Select the email you want to reply to in the Message pane.

2 Click Reply.

3 Type the message in the body pane.

4 Click Send.

HOT TIP: Mail offers formatting tools that you can use to change the font, font colour, font size and more.

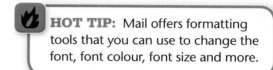

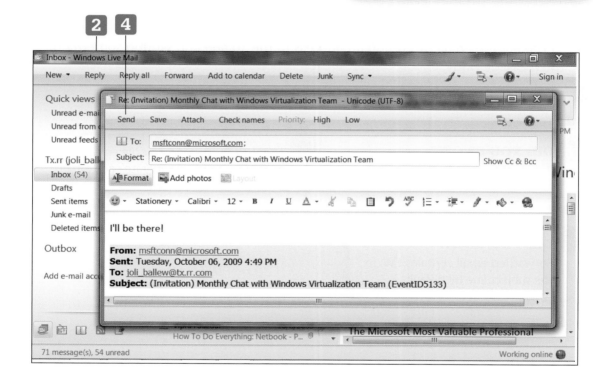

ALERT: If the email you are replying to was sent to you along with additional people, clicking Reply will send a reply to the person who composed the message. Clicking Reply all will send the reply to everyone who received the original email.

Forward an email

When someone sends you an email that you want to share with others, you forward the email. You do that by selecting the email and then clicking the Forward button.

1 Select the email you want to forward to in the Message pane.

2 Click Forward.

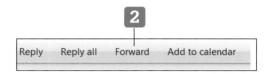

3 Complete the email by adding an address to the To line and writing something in the message body.

4 Click Send.

? DID YOU KNOW?
People often love to forward funny jokes.

HOT TIP: To send a single email to multiple recipients, separate each email address by a semicolon.

? DID YOU KNOW?
Forwarded email contains FW: in the subject line by default.

Compose and send a new email

You compose an email message by clicking New on the toolbar. You input who the email should be sent to, the subject, and then you type the message.

1 Click New.

2 Type the recipient's name or email address in the To line. If you want to add additional names, separate each email address by a semicolon.

3 Click Check names. This verifies the email address and puts a line under the address in the To line.

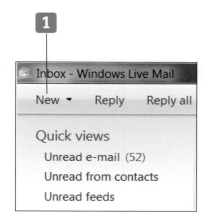

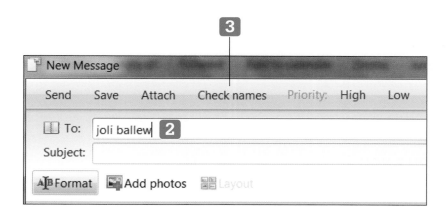

? DID YOU KNOW?

When working with email, make sure Mail is selected in the bottom left corner of the Live Mail Window. Other options include Calendar, Contacts, Feeds and Newsgroups.

🔥 HOT TIP: Click the address book icon next to the To line to add email addresses from your address book.

4 Type a subject in the Subject field.

5 Type the message in the body pane.

6 Click Send.

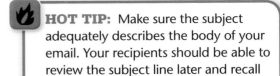

Attach something to an email using Attach

Although email that contains only a message serves its purpose quite a bit of the time, often you'll want to send a photograph, a short video, a sound recording, document or other data. When you want to add something to your message other than text, it's called adding an attachment. There are many ways to attach something to an email. One way is to use the Attach command.

1 Click New to create a new mail message.

2 Click Attach.

3 Locate the file to attach.

4 Double-click the file to attach.

 DID YOU KNOW?

If you are attaching photos and are prompted to send the photos in a 'photo email', clicking Yes will insert the pictures into the body of the email. Clicking No will attach them with the familiar paperclip, in essence on the 'outside' of the email.

ALERT: Anything you attach won't be removed from your computer; instead, a copy will be created for the attachment.

HOT TIP: When attaching (adding) files to an email, hold down the Ctrl key to select non-contiguous files, or the Shift key to select contiguous ones.

Attach a picture to an email using right-click

You can create an email that contains an attachment by right-clicking the file you want to attach. This method attaches the file(s) to a new email, which is fine *if you want to create a new email*. (It doesn't work with forwards or replies.) However, this method has a feature other methods don't. With this method, you can resize any images you've selected before sending them.

1 Locate the file you'd like to attach and right-click it.

2 Point to Send to.

3 Click Mail recipient.

4 If the item you're attaching is a picture, choose the picture size and click Attach. Note that you can opt to send the pictures in a photo email, where the image is inside the message body.

5 Complete the email and click Send.

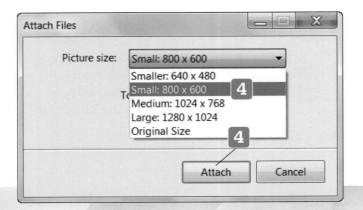

? DID YOU KNOW?
You can email from within applications, such as Microsoft Word or Excel. Generally, you'll find the desired option under the File menu, as a submenu of Send.

! ALERT: Avoid sending large attachments, especially to people that you know have a dial-up modem or those that get email only on a small device like a BlackBerry, iPhone or Mobile PC.

? DID YOU KNOW?
800 x 600 is usually the best option when sending pictures via email.

Insert a picture directly into the body of an email

Windows Live Mail lets you add images to the body of an email and edit them before sending. You can even put 'frames' around images, have Windows 'autocorrect' colour and brightness, and add more photos easily. This is called a photo email.

1 Click New to open a new email.

2 Click Add photos.

3 Browse to the photo(s) to add, and double-click them to add them.

4 Click any photo to add text, add a frame or rotate, among other options.

5 Complete the email, and when ready, click Send.

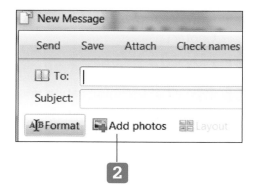

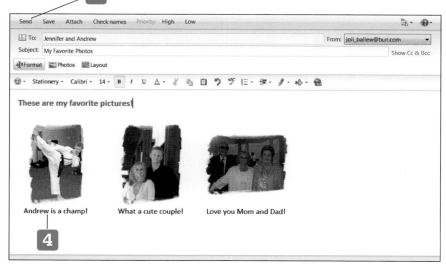

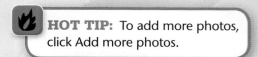

HOT TIP: To add more photos, click Add more photos.

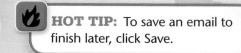

HOT TIP: To save an email to finish later, click Save.

Add a contact

A contact is a data file that holds the information you keep about a person. The contact information looks like a 'contact card', and the information can include a picture, email address, mailing address, first and last name, and similar data. You obtain contacts from various sources including people you email, people you instant message with Windows Live Messenger, and more.

1 From Windows Live Mail, click Contacts.

2 Click New.

3 Type all of the information you to add. Note that you can add information to each tab.

4 Click Add contact (not shown).

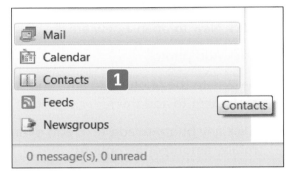

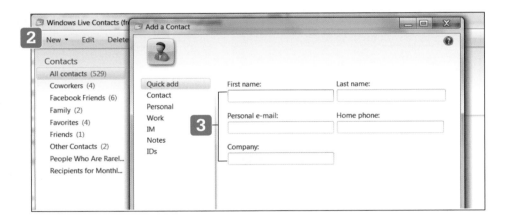

HOT TIP: Your contacts are stored in your Contacts folder inside your personal folder.

Print an email

Sometimes you'll need to print an email or its attachment. Print is not an option on the toolbar, though. You can add it by right-clicking the toolbar and selecting Customize toolbar. However, if you don't see a Print icon and you don't want to add one, you can click the Alt key on the keyboard, click File, and then click Print.

1 Select the email to print by clicking it in the Message pane.

2 Press Alt on the keyboard to show the Menu bar.

3 Click File, and click Print.

4 In the Print dialogue box, select the printer to use, if more than one exists.

5 Click Print.

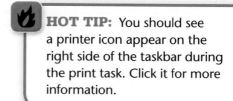

HOT TIP: On the keyboard, press Ctrl+P to print an email.

HOT TIP: You should see a printer icon appear on the right side of the taskbar during the print task. Click it for more information.

? DID YOU KNOW?

You can configure print preferences and choose what pages to print using Preferences. Refer to your printer's user manual to find out what print options your printer supports.

Apply a junk mail filter

Just as you receive unwanted information from insurance companies, radio stations and television ads, you're going to get unwanted advertisements in emails. This is referred to as junk email or 'spam'. Many of these advertisements are scams and rip-offs, and they can contain pornographic images. There are four filtering options in Windows Live Mail: No automatic filtering, Low, High, and Safe List Only.

1 Click the Menus icon and click Safety options.

WHAT DOES THIS MEAN?

No Automatic Filtering: Use this only if you do not want Windows Live Mail to block junk email messages. Windows Live Mail will continue to block messages from email addresses listed on the Blocked Senders list.

Low: Use this option if you receive very little junk email. You can start here and increase the filter if it becomes necessary.

High: Use this option if you receive a lot of junk email and want to block as much of it as possible. Also use this option for children's email accounts. Note that some valid email will probably be blocked, so you'll have to review the junk email folder occasionally, to make sure you aren't missing any email you want to keep.

Safe List Only: Use this option if you only want to receive messages from people or domain names on your Safe Senders list. This is a drastic step, and requires you add every sender you want to receive mail from to the Safe Senders list. Use this as a last resort.

2 From the Options tab, make a selection.

3 Click the Phishing tab.

4 Select Protect my Inbox from messages with potential Phishing links. Additionally, Move phishing E-mail to the junk e-mail folder.

5 Click OK.

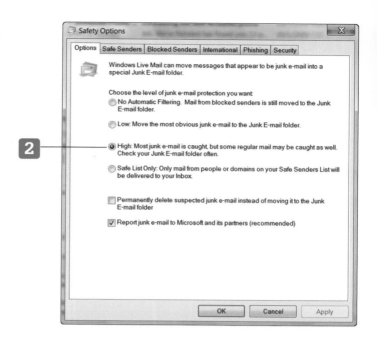

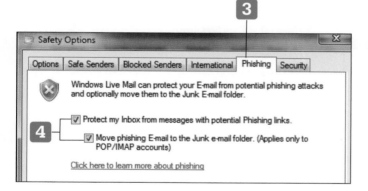

Create an email folder

It's important to perform some housekeeping chores once a month or so. If you don't, Windows Live Mail may bog down and perform slower than it should, or you may be unable to manage the email you want to keep. One way you can keep Mail under control is to create a new folder to hold email you want to keep and move mail into it.

1 Click the arrow next to New, and click Folder.

2 Type a name for the new folder.

3 Select any folder. The folder you create will appear underneath it.

4 Click OK.

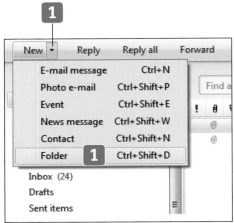

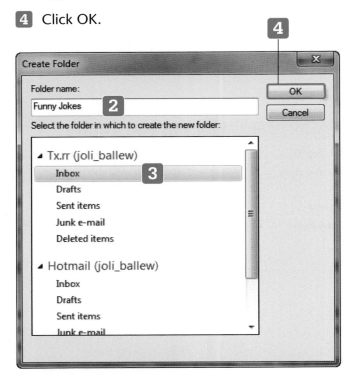

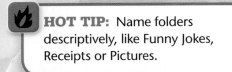

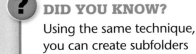

HOT TIP: Name folders descriptively, like Funny Jokes, Receipts or Pictures.

? DID YOU KNOW?
Using the same technique, you can create subfolders inside folders you create.

Move email to a folder

Moving an email from one folder (like your Inbox) to another (like Funny Jokes) is a simple task. Just drag the email from one folder to the other.

1 Right-click the email message to move in the message pane.

2 Hold the mouse button down while dragging the message to the new folder.

3 The email will no longer be in the Inbox, but will be in the new folder.

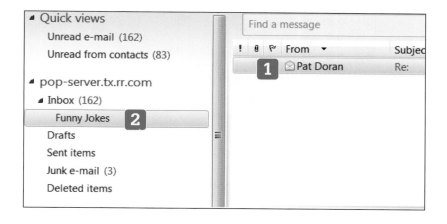

 HOT TIP: To access the email again, click the folder. The emails in that folder will appear in the Message pane.

Delete email in a folder

In order to keep Mail from getting bogged down, you'll need to delete email in folders often. Depending on how much email you get, this may be as often as once a week.

1 Right-click Junk e-mail.

2 Click Empty 'Junk e-mail' folder.

3 Similarly, right-click Deleted Items.

4 Click Empty 'Deleted Items' Folder.

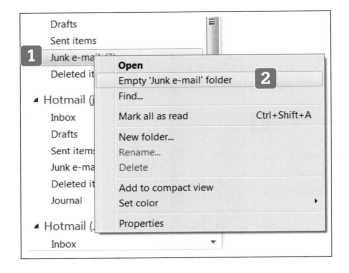

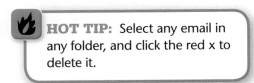

HOT TIP: Select any email in any folder, and click the red x to delete it.

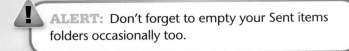

ALERT: Don't forget to empty your Sent items folders occasionally too.

10 Work with media

Introduction

Your Windows 7 computer comes with lots of ways to enjoy media. It includes Media Player to listen to and manage music, and Media Center for viewing Internet TV, pictures, videos and additional media types (like online media). With the required hardware, you can even watch live TV. It does not come with a photo-editing and management program though, but you've already worked with Windows Live Photo Gallery (Chapter 8), so you're all set!

Open Media Player and locate music

You open Media Player the same way you open other programs, from the Start menu. Once opened, you'll need to know where the Library button is, so you can access different kinds of media. We'll start with music.

1️⃣ Open Media Player from the taskbar.

2️⃣ Click the arrow next to the Library button.

3️⃣ Click Music.

? DID YOU KNOW?

Music is the default selection, but to be on the safe side, you should know how to change libraries. Did you notice Videos, Pictures, Recorded TV, Other Media and Playlists?

? DID YOU KNOW?

You can copy your CD collection easily. Just put any CD in the CD drive, and when prompted choose to copy the CD using Windows Media Player.

⚠ ALERT: The first time you start Windows Media Player, you'll be prompted to set it up. Choose Express to accept the default settings.

WHAT DOES THIS MEAN?

Windows Media Player: An application included with Windows 7. You can watch DVDs and videos here, listen to and manage music, and even listen to radio stations or view pictures.

Listen to a song

To play any music track, simply navigate to it and double-click it. Songs are listed in the 'Navigation' pane.

1 Open Media Player, if necessary, click the Library button and choose Music.

2 Click Album. (Note you can also click Artist or Genre too.)

3 Double-click any album to play it.

4 Double-click any song on the album to play it. Note the controls at the bottom of the screen.

> ► **SEE ALSO:** 'Open Media Player and locate music', previously.

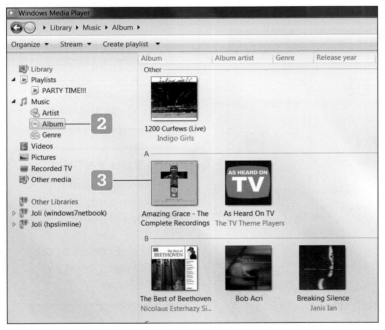

> **? DID YOU KNOW?**
> Media Player has Back and Forward buttons you can use to navigate Media Player.

> **? DID YOU KNOW?**
> The controls at the bottom of the screen from left to right are: Shuffle (to play songs in random order), Repeat, Stop, Previous, Play/Pause, Next, Mute, and a volume slider.

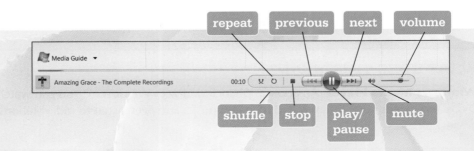

View pictures in Windows Live Photo Gallery

You can use various applications to view pictures with Windows 7, but Windows Live Photo Gallery is the best. With it, you have easy access to slide shows, editing tools and picture groupings. You can sort and filter, and organise as desired.

1 Open Windows Live Photo Gallery. If prompted, log in using your Windows Live ID.

2 Notice the sample pictures. Double-click any picture to open it in a larger window.

3 Click Back to gallery to return to the previous page (not shown).

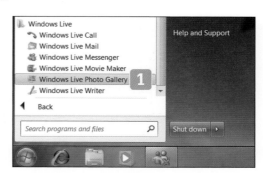

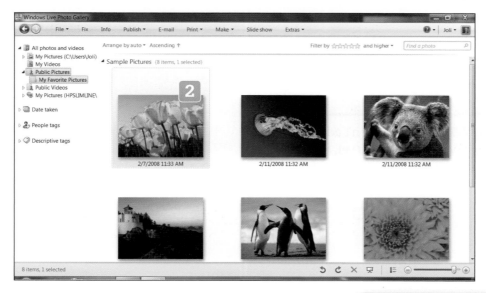

Play a slideshow of pictures

1 Open Windows Live Photo Gallery.

2 Select any folder that contains pictures.

3 Click the Slide Show button. Wait at least three seconds.

4 To end the show, press the Esc key on the keyboard.

HOT TIP: Press the F11 key on the keyboard to start a slideshow.

HOT TIP: If you haven't added any of your own photos yet, use the sample pictures to view a slideshow.

Auto adjust picture quality

With pictures now on your PC and available in Windows Live Photo Gallery, you can perform some editing. Photo Gallery offers the ability to correct brightness and contrast, colour temperature, tint and saturation, among other things.

1 Open Windows Live Photo Gallery.

2 Double-click a picture to edit.

3 Click Fix.

4 Click Auto adjust to fix problems with the photo. Adjustments will be made automatically.

5 Continue adjusting as desired, using the sliders to adjust the settings.

HOT TIP: When you select a 'fix' option, options will appear on the right side. You can apply the options as desired.

ALERT: After applying any option, to see more options, click the down and up arrows that will appear in the right pane.

HOT TIP: Click the Back to gallery button and your changes will be saved automatically.

Crop a picture

To crop means to remove parts of a picture you don't want.

1 Open Photo Gallery.

2 Select a picture to crop.

3 Click Fix.

4 Click Crop photo.

5 Drag the corners of the box to resize it, and drag the entire box to move it around in the picture.

6 Click Apply.

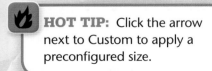 **HOT TIP:** Click the arrow next to Custom to apply a preconfigured size.

 **HOT TIP:** Click Rotate frame to change the position of the crop box.

Open Media Center

Before you open Media Center for the first time, make sure you have a working internet connection, speakers and a CD/DVD drive. To access all of the features, purchase and install a TV tuner. (Only then can you watch live TV.)

1 Click Start.

2 Click Windows Media Center. (If it's not in the Start menu, click All Programs.)

3 Use the arrow keys on the keyboard to view the interface icons.

? **DID YOU KNOW?**

Media Center's interface includes several menus: TV, Movies, Sports, Tasks, Extras, Pictures + Videos and Music.

? **DID YOU KNOW?**

Media Center is included with Windows 7 and allows you to watch live TV, among other media.

Explore Internet TV

If you like to watch TV, but your computer doesn't have a TV tuner, you have options. You can watch DVDs, your own videos, or Internet TV. Internet TV is under TV.

1 Open Media Center.

2 Use the arrow keys on your keyboard to locate TV, and Internet TV.

3 Click Install to access programming.

4 When installation completes, and this is a one-time task, browse programming options.

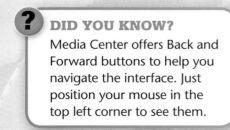

? DID YOU KNOW?

Media Center offers Back and Forward buttons to help you navigate the interface. Just position your mouse in the top left corner to see them.

View pictures in Media Center

You can view pictures in Photo Gallery and listen to music in Media Player, but you can do all of that in Media Center too. To view pictures, navigate to Pictures + Videos; for music, navigate to Music.

1 Open Media Center.

2 Use the arrow keys on the keyboard to locate Pictures + Videos.

3 Click Picture Library.

4 If you are connected to your home network, are prompted, and want to add pictures from other computers, click Add Pictures.

5 Work through the wizard to add the photos.

6 Select any photo folder to view its contents.

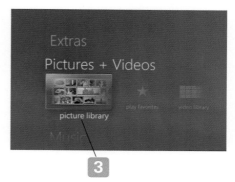

11 Connect to your home network

Introduction

If you have a home network, you will want to add your new Windows 7 computer to it. Once you've joined the computer you can use your computer to access shared resources like printers and folders, share media you've acquired on your computer, and access media that's on your home PC. You can use a network resource like a PC or external hard drive for backup too.

Create the connection

When you connect a new PC running Windows 7 to a wired network or get within range of a wireless one, Windows 7 will find the network and then ask you what kind of network it is. It's a public network if you're in a coffee shop, library or airport, and it's a private network if it's a network you manage, like one already in your home.

1 Connect physically to a wired network using an Ethernet cable or, if you have wireless hardware installed in your computer, get within range of a wireless network.

2 Select Home, Work, or Public network location.

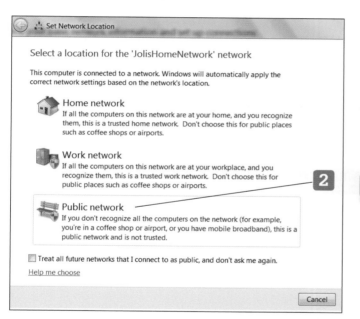

DID YOU KNOW?
Connecting to an existing network allows you to access shared features of the network. In a coffee shop that's probably only a connection to the internet; if it's a home network, it's your personal, shared data (and probably a connection to the internet too).

HOT TIP: When a network is accessible, either because you've connected to it using an Ethernet cable or through a wireless network card inside your PC, the Set Network Location wizard will appear.

WHAT DOES THIS MEAN?

Home: Choose this if the network is your home network or a network you trust (like a network at a friend's house). This connection type lets your computer *discover* other PCs, printers and devices on the network and they can see you.

Work: Choose this if you are connecting to a network at work. The settings for Work and Home are the same, only the titles differ so you can tell them apart easily.

Public location: Choose this if the network you want to connect to is open to anyone within range of it, like networks in coffee shops, airports and libraries. Windows 7 works out that if you choose Public, you only want to connect to the internet and nothing else. It closes down *discoverability*, so that even your shared data is safe.

Enable Network Discovery

Network Discovery tells Windows 7 that you're interested in seeing, and possibly joining, other networks. You can use a laptop to connect to a public network at a local café and you can use a desktop PC to connect to your own private network at home.

1 Open the Network and Sharing Center.

2 Notice the Network Map. It should show you are connected to a network and the internet.

3 In the Tasks pane, click Change advanced sharing settings.

ALERT: You will have to enable Network Discovery to be able to view and ultimately join available networks.

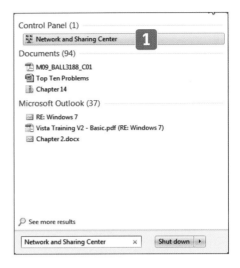

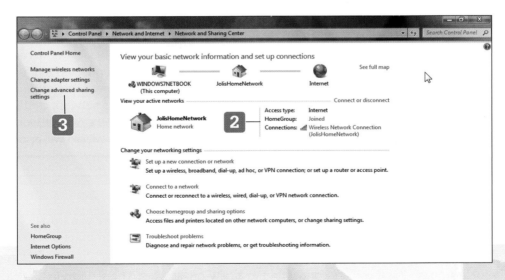

4 Click Turn on network discovery unless it is already turned on.

5 Click Save changes.

6 Click the X in the top right corner to close the Network and Sharing Center.

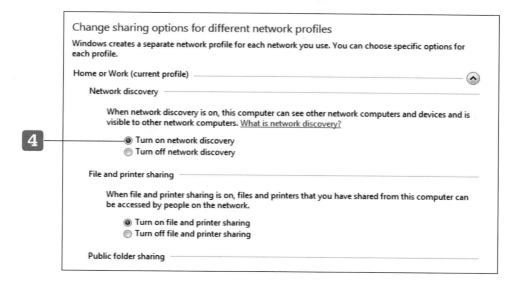

DID YOU KNOW?

The Network and Sharing Center is also where you set up file sharing, public folder sharing, printer sharing, password protected sharing and media sharing.

Verify sharing is enabled

When you tell Windows 7 you are joining a private network, like one at work or home, and you enable Network Discovery, certain sharing settings are configured. You need to see what sharing settings are configured and what are not. You can then decide exactly how and what you want to share with others on your network.

1 Open the Network and Sharing Center.

2 In the Tasks pane, click Change advanced sharing options.

3 Browse the sharing options. Turn on any options desired. You can turn on or turn off:

Control Panel Home

Manage wireless networks

Change adapter settings

2 ——Change advanced sharing settings

- ● File and printer sharing – files and printers on your computer that you have shared can be accessed by others on the network.

- ● Public folder sharing – public folders on your computer can be accessed by others on the network.

- ● Media streaming – media on your computer can be accessed by people and computers on the network. Your computer can also find media on the network.

- ● Password protected sharing – people who want to access your shared resources must have a user account and password to access it. If you turn this off, no validation is required.

- ● HomeGroup connections – if you have other Windows 7 PCs on your network, you can create a HomeGroup to more easily share data. Click to allow if this is the case.

4 Click Save changes.

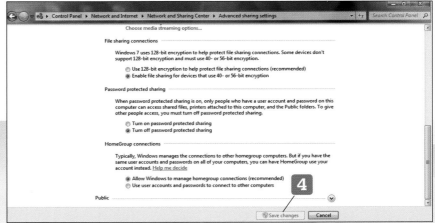

Access the Public folder

You can save data to the Public folder to share data easily with others on your network. You can access the Public folder by browsing to it. You can also browse the network for Public folders on other networked PCs. If you've created multiple accounts on your computer, every account holder can also access what's in the Public folder.

1 Click Start, and click Computer.

2 Double-click Local Disk (C:). (The letter you see here may differ.)

3 Double-click Users.

4 If you think you'll use the Public folder often, right-click it and choose Send to, Desktop (create shortcut).

Users

5 Double-click Public to open it.

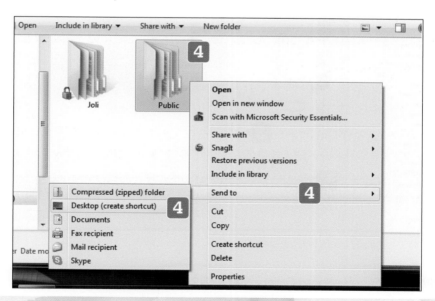

HOT TIP: If you create a shortcut to the Public folder on the desktop, the next time you want to access it, just open it from the desktop.

? **DID YOU KNOW?**

You can drag data from other open folders here to copy or move it. Right-click while dragging to have the option to move or copy.

Save data to the Public folder

If you've enabled Public folder sharing, you'll want to save data to share in the Public folders.

1 Open a picture, document, or other item you wish to save to the Pubic folders.

2 Click File, and click Save As.

3 In the Save As dialogue box, click Public (here it is a shortcut to the folder on the desktop)

4 Select the Public subfolder to save to.

5 Type a name for the file.

6 Click Save.

HOT TIP: Save pictures to the Public Pictures folder. Save documents to the Public Documents folder.

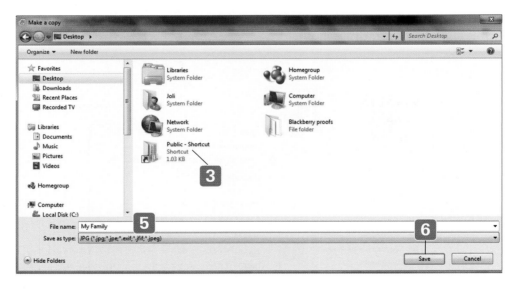

ALERT: In Windows Photo Gallery, you'll click File, and Make a Copy.

? **DID YOU KNOW?**
It's actually better to move data you want to share into the Public folders. That way, you won't create duplicate copies of the data on your hard drive.

HOT TIP: To move data, right-click it while dragging it to its new location. Click Move Here after dropping it, when prompted.

Share a personal folder

If you don't want to use the Public folders, you can share data directly from your own personal folders. To do this, you'll have to share the desired personal folders.

1 Locate the folder to share.

2 Right-click the folder.

3 Click Share with.

4 If you've created a homegroup, click the appropriate homegroup option. If not, choose Specific people.

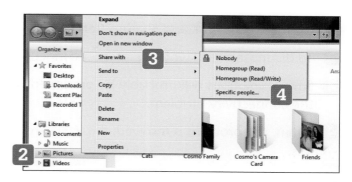

5 Type the name of the person to share the folder with and click Add. Repeat this step to add more people.

6 Click the arrow next to the new user name.

7 Select a sharing option.

8 Click Share.

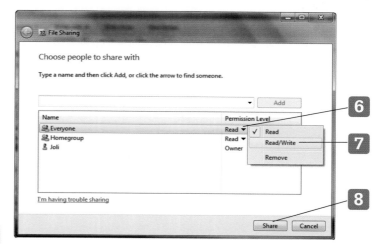

HOT TIP: You may want to share your own Pictures folder instead of copying or moving the files into the Public Pictures folder.

HOT TIP: To set up a homegroup, open the Network and Sharing Center and click Ready to Join next to Homegroup.

WHAT DOES THIS MEAN?

Owner: This is the person who created the file, uploaded the picture, purchased or ripped the music, or saved the video.

Read: This allows the user to access what's in the folder but that user cannot edit it.

Read/Write: This allows the user to access what's in the folder as well as edit it.

Diagnose connection problems

If you are having trouble connecting to the internet through a public or private network, you can diagnose internet problems using the Network and Sharing Center.

1 Open the Network and Sharing Center.

2 To diagnose a non-working internet connection, click the red x.

3 Several solutions will probably be presented. Click the first solution to try to resolve the connectivity problem.

4 Often, the problem is resolved. If it is not, move to the next step and the next until it is.

5 Click the X in the top right corner of the Network and Sharing Center window to close it.

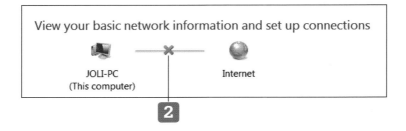

 ALERT: If you are connected to the internet, you will see a green line between your computer and the internet. If you are not connected you will see a red x.

 DID YOU KNOW?
There are additional troubleshooting tips in the Help and Support pages. Click Start, and click Help and Support.

12 Manage computer resources and connected devices

Introduction

Your computer uses its resources to function. It uses RAM (random access memory) to store data in the short term, a hard drive to store data in the long term, and a power supply to supply electrical power to the computer. While these things are 'internal', you'll also have resources that are 'external'. External resources include cameras, printers, scanners and the like. It's important that you know how to get the most from these resources and how to manage them. That's what you'll learn in this chapter.

Use ReadyBoost

ReadyBoost is a technology that lets you add more RAM (random access memory) to your computer easily, without opening the case. Adding RAM often improves performance dramatically. ReadyBoost lets you use a USB flash drive or a secure digital memory card (like the one in your digital camera), as RAM, if it meets certain requirements.

1 Insert a USB flash drive, thumb drive, portable music player or memory card into an available slot on the outside of your computer.

2 Wait while Windows 7 checks to see if the device can perform as memory.

3 If prompted to use the flash drive or memory card to improve system performance, click Speed up my system.

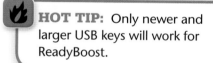

ALERT: USB keys must meet certain specifications, but don't worry about that, you'll be told if the hardware isn't up to par.

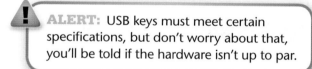

HOT TIP: Only newer and larger USB keys will work for ReadyBoost.

WHAT DOES THIS MEAN?

RAM: Random Access Memory. RAM is where information is stored temporarily so the operating system has quick access to it. The more RAM you have, the better your computer should perform.

USB or thumb drive: A small device that plugs into a USB port on your computer, often for the purpose of backing up or storing files on external media.

Portable music player: Often a small USB drive. This device also has a headphone jack and controls for listening to music stored on it.

Media card: A removable card used in digital cameras to store data and transfer it to the computer.

Use Disk Defragmenter

Your computer uses its hard disk drive to store data permanently, or until you delete it. Files can become 'fragmented' when their data isn't stored together on the hard disk. You can defragment the data on the drive to improve performance.

1 Click Start, and type Defrag.

2 Under Programs, click Disk Defragmenter.

3 Verify that Disk Defragmenter is configured to run automatically. If it is not, click Configure schedule.

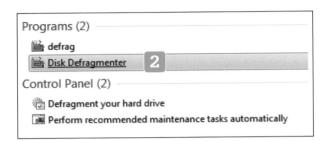

4 If you clicked Configure schedule in step 3, choose the desired settings in the resulting window. It's best to run this program once a week. Click OK.

5 Click Close.

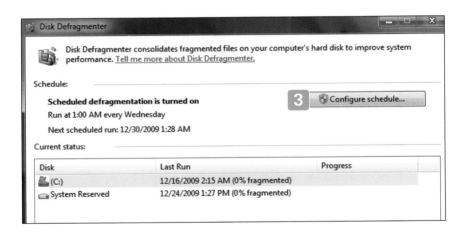

? DID YOU KNOW?

Windows 7 defragments your disk automatically, but it's best to ensure this feature is enabled and running properly.

? DID YOU KNOW?

To see how the files on your hard disk are stored, click Analyze disk.

Change when your computer sleeps

Your computer is configured to go to sleep after a specific period of idle time. You can change how long the computer is idle before going into sleep mode from the Power Options window.

1 Click Start, and in the Start Search window type Power.

2 In the results, under Control Panel, click Power Options.

3 Click Change when the computer sleeps.

4 Use the drop-down lists to make changes as desired.

5 Click Save changes.

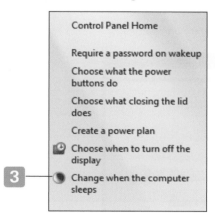

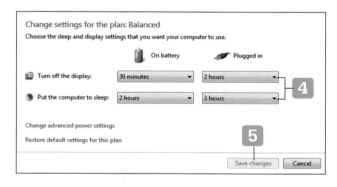

ALERT: You won't see the options for a battery on a desktop PC.

? DID YOU KNOW?
You can restore the sleep defaults by clicking Restore default settings for this plan.

🔥 HOT TIP: When you change the options here, the changes are applied to the currently selected plan, in this case, Balanced.

Change what happens when you press the Power button or close the lid

Your computer is configured to do something specific when you press the Power button and when you close a laptop's lid. To view the default behaviour and change it if desired, look to the Power Options window once more.

1 Click Start, and in the Start Search window type Power.

2 In the results, under Programs, click Power Options.

3 Click Choose what the power buttons do.

4 Use the drop-down lists to make changes as desired.

5 Click Save changes.

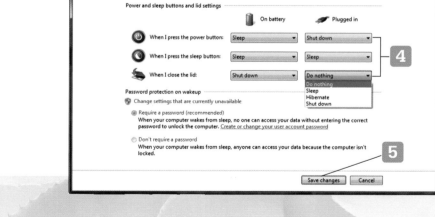

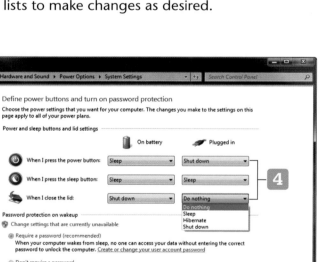

ALERT: Always shut down the computer when you aren't going to use it for a few days.

HOT TIP: You can change the settings so that pressing the Power button causes the computer to go to sleep.

Manage all connected devices

There's one place you can view and manage all of your connected devices. From there, you can see what's working and what isn't, what's connected and what isn't, and what devices, like printers, are configured as default devices.

1 Click Start.

2 Click Devices and Printers. (Some people call this window 'Device Stage'.)

3 Review the hardware; double-click any device to view or edit its properties.

green tick mark

 HOT TIP: A green tick mark indicates a default device. In the case of a printer, it's the device that will be used if no specific information is offered.

13 Stay Secure

Introduction

Windows 7 comes with a lot of built-in features to keep you, your computer and your data safe. Windows 7 security tools and features help you avoid email scams, harmful websites and hackers, and also helps you protect your data and your computer from unscrupulous co-workers or nosy family members. If you know how to take advantage of the available safeguards, you'll be protected in almost all cases. You just need to be aware of the dangers, heed (and resolve) security warnings when they are given and use all of the available features in Windows 7 to protect yourself and your PC.

Add a new user account

You created your user account when you first turned on your new Windows 7 PC. Your user account is what defines your personal folders as well as your settings for desktop background, screen saver and other items. You are the 'administrator' of your computer. If you share the PC with someone, they should have their own user account too.

1 Click Start.

2 Click Control Panel.

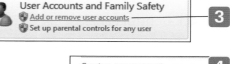

3 Click Add or remove user accounts.

4 Click Create a new account.

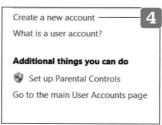

5 Type a new account name, verify Standard user is selected, and click Create Account.

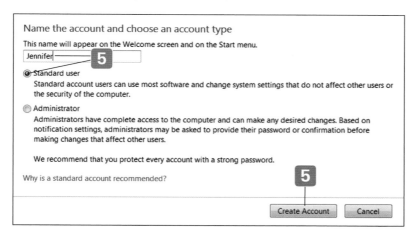

! **ALERT:** All accounts should have a password applied to them. Refer to the next section 'Require a password'.

! **ALERT:** If every person who accesses your PC has their own standard user account and password, and if every person logs on using that account and then logs off the PC each time they're finished using it, you'll never have to worry about anyone accessing anyone else's personal data.

? **DID YOU KNOW?**
Administrators can make changes to system-wide settings but Standard users cannot (without an administrator's user name and password).

Require a password

All user accounts, even yours, should be password-protected. When a password is configured, you must type the password to log on to your PC or laptop. This protects the PC from unauthorised access.

1 Click Start.

2 Click Control Panel.

3 Add or remove user accounts.

4 Click the user account to apply a password to.

5 Click Create a password.

6 Type the new password, type it again to confirm it, and type a password hint.

7 Click Create password.

Make changes to Jennifer's account

Change the account name
Create a password ———— **5**
Change the picture
Set up Parental Controls
Change the account type
Delete the account

Manage another account

Jennifer
Standard user

Create a password for Jennifer's account

Jennifer
Standard user

You are creating a password for Jennifer.

If you do this, Jennifer will lose all EFS-encrypted files, personal certificates and stored passwords for Web sites or network resources.

To avoid losing data in the future, ask Jennifer to make a password reset floppy disk.

New password
Confirm new password

If the password contains capital letters, they must be typed the same way every time.
How to create a strong password

6

Type a password hint

The password hint will be visible to everyone who uses this computer.
What is a password hint?

7

Create password   Cancel

ALERT: Create a password that contains upper- and lower-case letters and a few numbers. Write the password down and keep it somewhere out of sight and safe.

DID YOU KNOW?
When you need to make a system-wide change, you have to be logged on as an administrator or type an administrator's user name and password.

Configure Windows Update

It's very important to configure Windows Update to get and install updates automatically. This is the easiest way to ensure your computer is as up-to-date as possible, at least as far as patching any security flaws Microsoft uncovers, having access to the latest features, and obtaining updates to the operating system itself. I propose you verify that the recommended settings are enabled as detailed here, and occasionally check for optional updates manually.

1 Click Start.

2 Click Control Panel.

3 Click System and Security.

4 Under Windows Update, click Turn automatic updating on or off.

5 Configure the settings as shown here or verify settings are similar, and click OK.

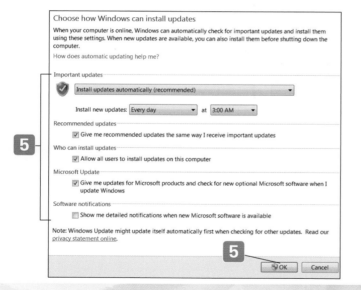

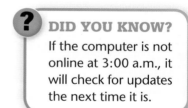

? DID YOU KNOW?
If the computer is not online at 3:00 a.m., it will check for updates the next time it is.

! ALERT: You may see that optional components or updates are available. You can view these updates and install them if desired.

WHAT DOES THIS MEAN?

Windows Update: If enabled and configured properly, when you are online, Windows 7 will check for security updates automatically, and install them. You don't have to do anything, and your PC is always updated with the latest security patches and features.

Scan for viruses with Windows Defender

You don't have to do much to Windows Defender except understand that it offers protection against internet threats like malware. It's enabled by default and it runs in the background. However, if you ever think your computer has been attacked by an internet threat (malware, etc.) you can run a manual scan here.

1 Open Windows Defender. (Click Start, type Defender, and in the results click Windows Defender.)

2 Click the arrow next to Scan (not the Scan icon). Click Full scan if you think the computer has been infected.

3 Click the X in the top right corner to close the Windows Defender window.

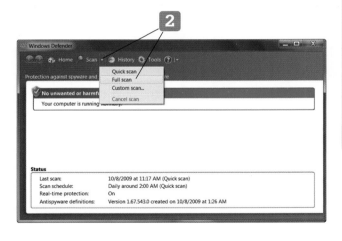

WHAT DOES THIS MEAN?

Malware: Stands for malicious software. Malware includes viruses, worms, spyware, etc.

Enable the firewall

Windows Firewall is a software program that checks the data that comes in from the internet (or a local network) and then decides whether it's good data or bad. If it deems the data harmless, it will allow it to come though the firewall, if not, it's blocked.

1 Click Start, and in the Start Search window type Firewall.

2 Click Windows Firewall.

3 The firewall should be enabled, as shown here.

Control Panel (4)

- Windows Firewall **2**
- Allow a program through Windows Firewall
- Check firewall status
- Check security status

4 If it is not enabled:

- From the left pane, click Turn Windows Firewall on or off.

- Select Turn on Windows Firewall. Than review your other settings.

- Click OK.

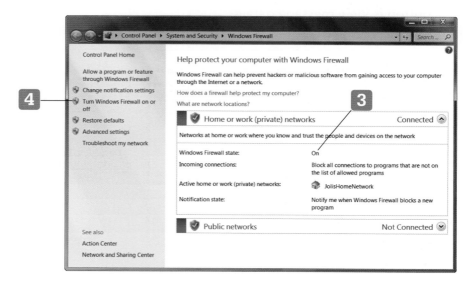

ALERT: You have to have a firewall to keep hackers from getting access to your PC, and to help prevent your computer from sending out malicious code if it is ever attacked by a virus or worm.

View and resolve Action Center warnings

Windows 7 tries hard to take care of your PC and your data. You'll see a pop-up if your anti-virus software is out of date (or not installed), if you don't have the proper security settings configured, or if Windows Update or the firewall is disabled. You'll also get a user account control prompt each time you want to install a program or make system-wide changes.

1 In the taskbar, click the icon that looks like a flag.

2 Click Open Action Center.

3 If there's anything in red or yellow, click the down arrow (if necessary), to see the problem.

4 Click the suggestion button to view the resolution and perform the task. In this case, the button is View message details.

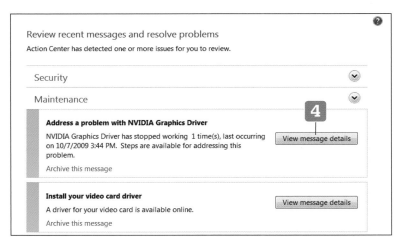

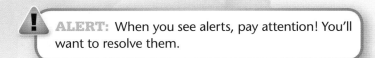

ALERT: When you see alerts, pay attention! You'll want to resolve them.

5 Perform the task.

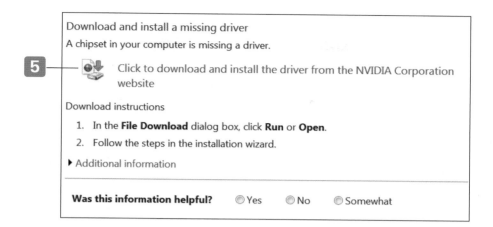

Download and install a missing driver

A chipset in your computer is missing a driver.

5 Click to download and install the driver from the NVIDIA Corporation website

Download instructions

1. In the **File Download** dialog box, click **Run** or **Open**.
2. Follow the steps in the installation wizard.

▶ Additional information

Was this information helpful? ⊙ Yes ⊙ No ⊙ Somewhat

WHAT DOES THIS MEAN?

Virus: A self-replicating program that infects computers with intent to do harm. Viruses often come in the form of an attachment to an email.

Worm: A self-replicating program that infects computers with intent to do harm. However, unlike a virus, it does not need to attach itself to a running program.

 ALERT: Install anti-virus software to protect your PC from viruses and worms.

 DID YOU KNOW? Windows 7 comes with malware protection but not anti-virus protection.

Create a basic backup

Windows 7 comes with a backup program you can use to back up your personal data. The backup program is called Backup and Restore.

1 Open Backup and Restore. (Click Start, type Backup.)

2 If you have performed a backup before, click Back up now. Wait while the backup completes.

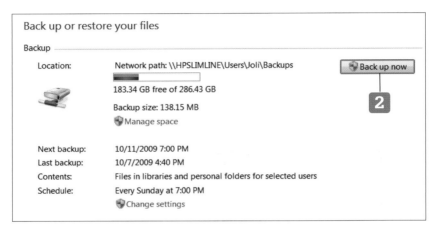

3 If you've never created a backup, click Set up backup.

- Decide on a place to save your backup.
- Click Save on a network and choose a location if desired.
- Select the backup destination.
- Click Next.

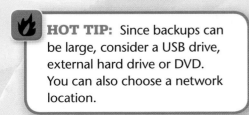

HOT TIP: Since backups can be large, consider a USB drive, external hard drive or DVD. You can also choose a network location.

4 Select Let Windows choose (recommended). Click Next.

5 Wait while the backup completes.

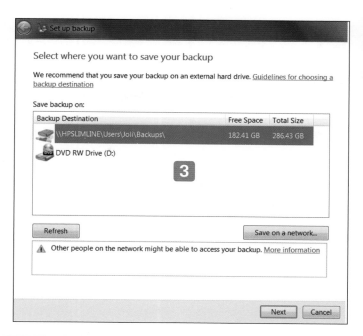

4

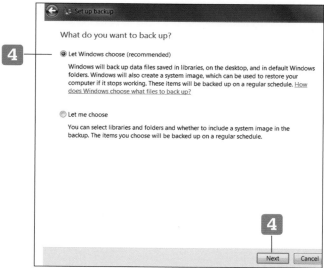

14 Fix problems

Introduction

When problems arise, you will want to resolve them quickly. Windows 7 offers plenty of help. System Restore can fix problems automatically by 'restoring' your computer to an earlier time. If the boot-up process is slow, you can disable unwanted start-up items with the System Configuration tool. Additionally, you can use the Network and Sharing Center to help you resolve connectivity problems and use Device Manager to 'roll back' a driver that didn't work, and if your computer seems bogged down, you can delete unwanted programs and files easily.

Use System Restore

System Restore regularly creates and saves *restore points* that contain information about your computer that Windows uses to work properly. If your computer starts acting oddly, you can use System Restore to restore your computer to a time when it was functioning correctly.

1 Open System Restore.

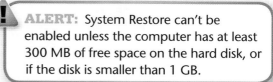

ALERT: System Restore can't be enabled unless the computer has at least 300 MB of free space on the hard disk, or if the disk is smaller than 1 GB.

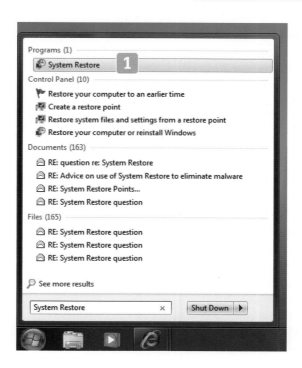

Programs (1)
🎧 System Restore   **1**

Control Panel (10)
🚩 Restore your computer to an earlier time
🖥 Create a restore point
🖥 Restore system files and settings from a restore point
🎧 Restore your computer or reinstall Windows

Documents (163)
📨 RE: question re: System Restore
📨 RE: Advice on use of System Restore to eliminate malware
📨 RE: System Restore Points...
📨 RE: System Restore question

Files (165)
📨 RE: System Restore question
📨 RE: System Restore question
📨 RE: System Restore question

🔎 See more results

System Restore   ✕   Shut Down ▶

WHAT DOES THIS MEAN?

Restore point: A snapshot of the Registry and system state that can be used to make an unstable computer stable again.

Registry: A part of the operating system that contains information about hardware configuration and settings, user configuration and preferences, software configuration and preferences, and other system-specific information.

2 Click Next to accept and apply the recommended restore point.

3 Click Finish.

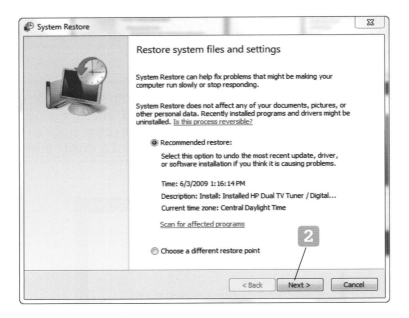

🔥 **HOT TIP:** Many problems occur due to loose or disconnected cables. A mouse can't work unless it's plugged in or its wireless component is. A cable modem can't work unless it's connected securely to the computer and the wall. When troubleshooting, always check your connections.

⚠️ **ALERT:** If you are running System Restore on a computer, make sure it's plugged it. System Restore should never be interrupted.

❓ **DID YOU KNOW?**
Because System Restore works only with its own system files, running System Restore will not affect any of your personal data. Your pictures, email, documents, music, etc. will not be deleted or changed.

Disable unwanted start-up items

Lots of programs and applications start when you boot your computer. This causes the start-up process to take longer than it should, and programs that start also run in the background, slowing down computer performance. You should disable unwanted start-up items to improve all-around performance.

1 Click Start.

2 In the Start Search window, type System Configuration.

3 Under Programs, click System Configuration.

4 From the Startup tab, deselect third-party programs you recognise but do not use daily.

5 Click OK.

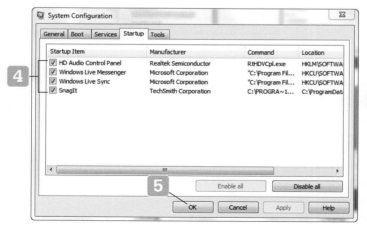

? DID YOU KNOW?
Even if you disable a program from starting when Windows does, you can start it when you need it by clicking it in the Start and All Programs menu.

! ALERT: Do not deselect anything you don't recognise, or the operating system!

! ALERT: You'll have to restart the computer to apply the changes.

🔥 HOT TIP: If you see a long list under the System Configuration's Startup tab, go through it carefully and consider uninstalling unwanted programs from the Control Panel.

Resolve internet connectivity problems

When you have a problem connecting to your local network or to the internet, you can often resolve the problem in the Network and Sharing Center.

1 Open the Network and Sharing Center.

2 Click the red x.

3 Perform the steps in the order they are presented.

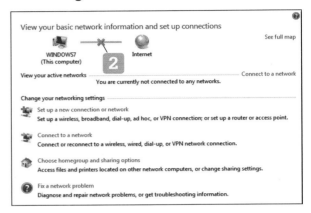

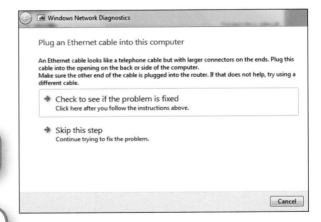

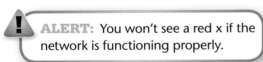

ALERT: You won't see a red x if the network is functioning properly.

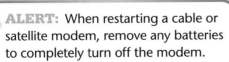

ALERT: When restarting a cable or satellite modem, remove any batteries to completely turn off the modem.

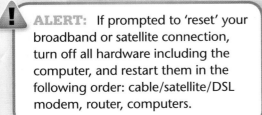

ALERT: If prompted to 'reset' your broadband or satellite connection, turn off all hardware including the computer, and restart them in the following order: cable/satellite/DSL modem, router, computers.

 DID YOU KNOW?

Most of the time, performing the first step will resolve your network problem.

Use Roll Back Driver

If you download and install a new driver for a piece of hardware and it doesn't work properly, you can use Device Driver Rollback to return to the previously installed driver.

1 Click Start.

2 Right-click Computer.

3 Click Properties.

4 Under Tasks, click Device Manager (not shown).

5 Click the + sign next to the hardware that uses the driver to roll back. It will change to a minus sign.

6 Double-click the device name.

7 Click the Driver tab and click Roll Back Driver.

8 Click OK.

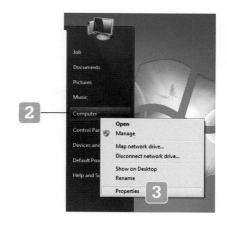

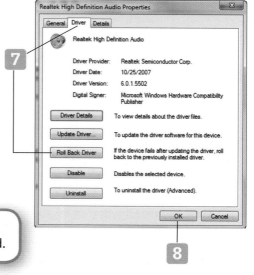

ALERT: The Roll Back Driver option will only be available if a new driver has recently been installed.

ALERT: You can only roll back to the previous driver. This means that if you have a driver (D), and then install a new driver (D1) and it doesn't work, and then you install another driver (D2) and it doesn't work, using Device Driver Rollback will revert to D1, not the driver (D) before it.

View available hard drive space

Problems can occur when hard drive space gets too low. This can become a problem when you use a computer to record television shows or films (these require a lot of hard drive space), store videos from a video camera, or if your hard drive is partitioned.

1 Click Start.

2 Click Computer.

3 In the Computer window, right-click the C: drive and choose Properties.

4 View the available space.

 ALERT: If you find you are low on disk space, you'll have to delete unnecessary files and/or applications.

 ALERT: If the drive is more than 85% full, delete or move some of the data on it, if possible.

▶ **SEE ALSO:** 'Move a file', 'Delete a file', 'Move a folder' and 'Delete a folder', all in Chapter 4.

WHAT DOES THIS MEAN?

Partition: Some hard drives are configured to have multiple sections, called partitions. The C: partition may have 20 GB available, while the D: partition may have 60 GB. If you save everything to the C: partition (failing to use the D: partition), it can get full quickly.

Uninstall unwanted programs

If you haven't used an application in more than a year, you probably never will. You can uninstall unwanted programs from the Control Panel.

1 Click Start, click Control Panel.

2 In Control Panel, click Uninstall a program.

3 Scroll through the list. Click a program name if you want to uninstall it.

4 Click Uninstall.

5 Follow the prompts to uninstall the program.

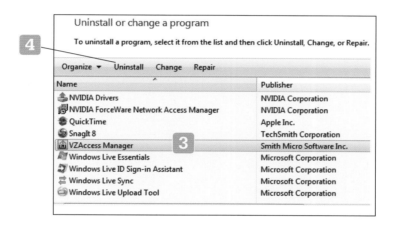

 HOT TIP: Look for programs in the list that start with the name of the manufacturer of your computer (Acer, Hewlett-Packard, Dell, etc.).

 ALERT: Your computer may have come with programs you don't even know about. Perform these steps to find out what's on it.

Top 10 Computer Basics Problems Solved

Problem 1: A technician is asking for my computer's specs

There may come a time where you have to speak to a tech-savvy friend, Internet Service Provider (ISP) representative or other help desk technician. Those people will ask the same questions: 'What edition of Windows 7 are you running?', 'How much RAM do you have?'; 'Is there anything called out in Device Manager, denoting a problem with your hardware?' Here's how to find the answer to those questions.

1 Click Start and locate Computer.

2 Right-click Computer and click Properties.

3 Review the information in the System window, including the Windows edition and amount of RAM.

4 Click Device Manager.

5 Note any 'unknown devices'. These devices are not currently recognised by Windows 7. A technician or tech-savvy friend can help you resolve any errors here.

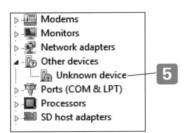

HOT TIP: Click Windows Experience Score to learn more about the hardware installed inside your computer.

HOT TIP: Click the red X in the top right corner of the System window to make it disappear (i.e. to close the window).

Problem 2: I can't locate the program I want to use

To locate a program on your computer you can search for it using the Start Search window. Just type in what you want, and select the appropriate program from the list.

1 Click Start.

2 In the Start Search window, type Photo.

3 Note the results.

4 Click any result to open it. If you want to open Windows Live Photo Gallery, click it once. Note that it's under Programs.

 DID YOU KNOW?

This feature became available in Windows Vista and is included with Windows 7, but was not available in Windows XP.

ALERT: When you search using the Start Search window, all kinds of results may appear, not just programs.

 HOT TIP: The easiest way to find something on your computer is to type it into this search window, and that includes files, folders, photos, music, pictures and videos.

Problem 3: People are using my computer and accessing my data

You created your user account when you first turned on your new Windows 7 PC. Your user account is what defines your personal folders as well as your settings for desktop background, screen saver and other items. You are the 'administrator' of your computer. If you share the PC with someone, they should have their own user account too.

1 Click Start.

2 Click Control Panel.

3 Click Add or remove user accounts.

4 Click Create a new account.

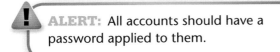

ALERT: All accounts should have a password applied to them.

? DID YOU KNOW?

Administrators can make changes to system-wide settings but Standard users cannot (without an Administrator's user name and password).

5 Type a new account name, verify Standard user is selected, and click Create Account.

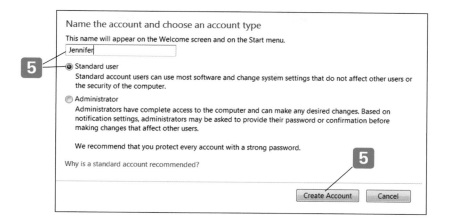

Name the account and choose an account type

This name will appear on the Welcome screen and on the Start menu.

Jennifer

5 ● Standard user

Standard account users can use most software and change system settings that do not affect other users or the security of the computer.

○ Administrator

Administrators have complete access to the computer and can make any desired changes. Based on notification settings, administrators may be asked to provide their password or confirmation before making changes that affect other users.

We recommend that you protect every account with a strong password.

Why is a standard account recommended?

5

Create Account   Cancel

? DID YOU KNOW?

Once the account is created you can also click Change the picture, Change the account name, Create a password (Remove the password) and other options to further personalise the account.

! ALERT: If every person who accesses your PC has their own standard user account and password, and if every person logs on using that account and then logs off the PC each time they're finished using it, you'll never have to worry about anyone accessing anyone else's personal data.

Problem 4: I might have a virus, malware or spyware

Windows Defender offers protection against internet threats like malware. It's enabled by default and it runs in the background. However, if you ever think your computer has been attacked by an internet threat (virus, malware, spyware, etc.) you can run a manual scan here.

1 Open Windows Defender. (Click Start, type Defender, and in the results click Windows Defender.)

2 Click the arrow next to Scan (not the Scan icon). Click Full scan if you think the computer has been infected.

3 Click the X in the top right corner to close the Windows Defender window.

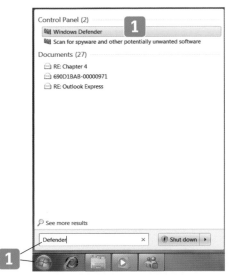

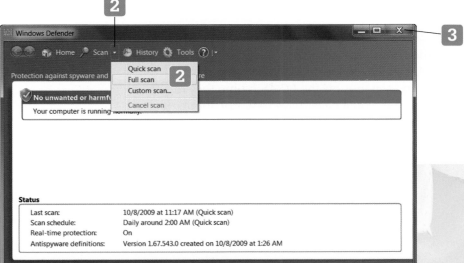

Problem 5: I keep seeing pop-ups that there's something wrong with my PC

Windows 7 tries hard to take care of your PC and your data. You'll see a pop-up if your anti-virus software is out of date (or not installed), if you don't have the proper security settings configured, or if Windows Update or the firewall is disabled. You'll also get a user account control prompt each time you want to install a program or make system wide changes.

1 In the taskbar, click the icon that looks like a flag.

2 Click Open Action Center.

3 If there's anything in red or yellow, click the down arrow (if necessary), to see the problem.

4 Click the suggestion button to view the resolution. In this case, the button is View message details.

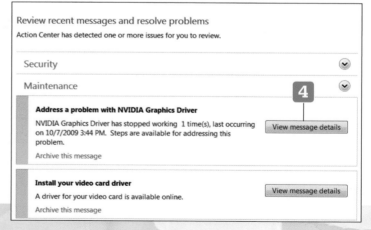

5 Perform the task.

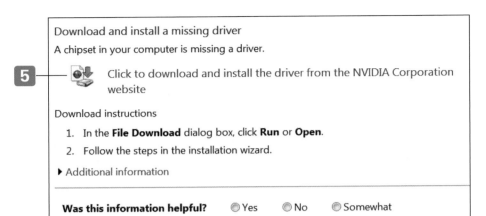

Download and install a missing driver

A chipset in your computer is missing a driver.

Click to download and install the driver from the NVIDIA Corporation website

Download instructions

1. In the **File Download** dialog box, click **Run** or **Open**.
2. Follow the steps in the installation wizard.

▶ Additional information

Was this information helpful?   ⦿ Yes   ⦿ No   ⦿ Somewhat

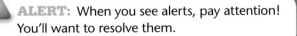

! ALERT: When you see alerts, pay attention! You'll want to resolve them.

 DID YOU KNOW? Windows 7 comes with malware protection but not anti-virus protection.

Problem 6: I'm connected to a network, or within range of a wireless one, but I can't even see it to connect

Network Discovery tells Windows 7 that you're interested in seeing, and possibly joining, other networks. If you're interested in joining a network, you'll have to tell Windows 7.

1 Open the Network and Sharing Center.

2 In the Tasks pane, click Change advanced sharing settings.

Change advanced sharing settings

3 Click Turn on network discovery unless it is already turned on.

4 Click Save changes.

5 Click the X to close the Network and Sharing Center.

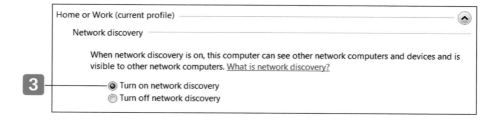

 ALERT: You will have to enable Network Discovery to be able to view and ultimately join available networks.

? DID YOU KNOW?
The Network and Sharing Center is also where you set up file sharing, public folder sharing, printer sharing, password protected sharing and media sharing.

Problem 7: Others on my network can't view my shared data

When you tell Windows 7 you are joining a private network, like one at work or home, and you enable Network Discovery, certain sharing settings are configured. You need to see what sharing settings are configured and what are not. You can then decide exactly how and what you want to share with others on your network.

1 Open the Network and Sharing Center.

2 In the Tasks pane, click Change advanced sharing settings.

3 Browse the sharing options. Turn on any options desired. You can turn on or turn off:

Control Panel Home

Manage wireless networks

Change adapter settings

2 Change advanced sharing settings

- File and printer sharing – files and printers on your computer that you have shared can be accessed by others on the network.

- Public folder sharing – public folders on your computer can be accessed by others on the network.

- Media streaming – media on your computer can be accessed by people and computers on the network. Your computer can also find media on the network.

- Password protected sharing – people who want to access your shared resources must have a user account and password to access it. If you turn this off, no validation is required.

- HomeGroup connections – if you have other Windows 7 PCs on your network, you can create a homegroup to share data more easily. Click to allow if this is the case.

File and printer sharing

When file and printer sharing is on, files and printers that you have shared from this computer can be accessed by people on the network.

3

- ◉ Turn on file and printer sharing
- ○ Turn off file and printer sharing

Public folder sharing

When Public folder sharing is on, people on the network, including homegroup members, can access files in the Public folders. What are the Public folders?

- ◉ Turn on sharing so anyone with network access can read and write files in the Public folders
- ○ Turn off Public folder sharing (people logged on to this computer can still access these folders)

Media streaming

When media streaming is on, people and devices on the network can access pictures, music, and videos on this computer. This computer can also find media on the network.

Media streaming is on.
Choose media streaming options...

4 Click Save changes.

Problem 8: I could connect to the internet yesterday, but today I can't

If you are having trouble connecting to the internet through a public or private network, you can diagnose internet problems using the Network and Sharing Center.

1 Open the Network and Sharing Center.

2 To diagnose a non-working internet connection, click the red x.

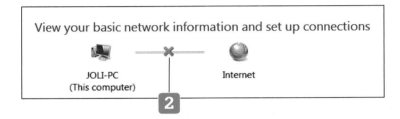

View your basic network information and set up connections

JOLI-PC
(This computer)

Internet

2

3 Several solutions will probably be presented. Click the first solution to try to resolve the connectivity problem.

4 Often, the problem is resolved. If it is not, move to the next step and the next until it is.

5 Click the X in the top right corner of the Network and Sharing window to close it.

 ALERT: If you are connected to the internet, you will see a green line between your computer and the internet. If you are not connected you will see a red x.

 DID YOU KNOW?
There are additional troubleshooting tips in the Help and Support pages. Click Start, and then click Help and Support.

Problem 9: I've uploaded some pictures to my computer and I want to improve their quality

With pictures now on your PC and available in Windows Live Photo Gallery, you can perform some editing. Photo Gallery offers the ability to correct brightness and contrast, colour temperature, tint and saturation, among other things.

1 Open Windows Live Photo Gallery.

2 Double-click a picture to edit.

3 Click Fix.

4 Click Auto adjust to fix problems with the photo. Adjustments will be made automatically.

5 Continue adjusting as desired, using the sliders to adjust the settings.

HOT TIP: Click the Back to Gallery button and your changes will be saved automatically.

ALERT: After applying any option, to see more options, click the down and up arrows that will appear in the right pane.

HOT TIP: When you select a 'fix' option, options will appear on the right side. You can apply the options as desired.

Problem 10: I can't find any email, photo editing or instant messaging program

Windows Live Essentials contains all of the programs you'll need to manage email, instant message with contacts, edit photos, and even create and edit your own movies. You can choose to install additional applications from the suite too, including the Internet Explorer toolbar that connects all of this together seamlessly.

1 Open Internet Explorer and go to http://download.live.com/.

2 Look for the Download button and click it. You'll be prompted to click Download once more on the next screen.

3 Click Run, and when prompted, click Yes.

4 When prompted, select the items to download. You can select all of the items or only some of them. (Make sure to at least select Live Mail and Live Photo Gallery.)

5 Click Install.

6 When prompted to select your settings, make the desired choices. You can't go wrong here; there are no bad options.

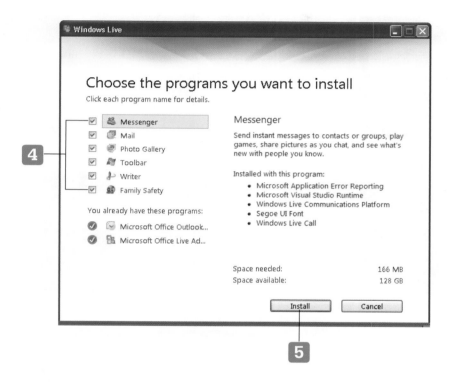

HOT TIP: Select Mail, Photo Gallery and Toolbar, for best results. You'll probably use all three.

DID YOU KNOW?
It's OK to select all of these programs if you think you'll use them; they are all free.

USE YOUR COMPUTER
WITH CONFIDENCE

9780273723486

9780273723493

9780273723479

9780273723523

9780273723530

9780273723509

9780273723547

9780273723554

9780273729136

9780273729297

9780273729181

9780273729129

9780273729174

Practical. Simple. Fast.

in Simple steps

PEARSON